The Church

"A Mystery Revealed"

by Turnel Nelson

PUBLISHING

The Church

by Turnel Nelson

Published by:

PUBLISHING

All Scripture quotations, unless noted otherwise, are from the Holy Bible, King James Version.

All rights reserved. No part of this book may be reproduced in any form without permission in writing from the publisher, except in the case of brief quotations embodied in church related publications, critical articles or reviews.

Printed in the United States of America

ISBN 1-56229-431-8

Copyright © 1994
by Turnel J. Nelson

Pneuma Life Publishing
P.O. Box 10612
Bakersfield, CA 93389
(805) 837-2113

Contents

Dedication
Introduction

Dedication

This book is dedicated to my wonderful wife, Joycelyn, for her love and support in 29 years of ministry. Many more to come.

Introduction

Contrary to the popular and present image of the Church as a religious entity known as Christianity, God's purpose and intent for the Church is that it be an international embassy on earth which represents and manifests the policies, dictates, and purposes of the Kingdom of God.

As born again believers in the Lord Jesus Christ, we are not merely members or constituents of a religion; but we are, in actuality, citizens of the divine nation known biblically as the Kingdom of God or Kingdom of Heaven. The Apostle Paul declares that those who God has called as leadership in the body of Christ, (namely those who are elders in the Church), have been trusted with the responsibility of being ambassadors for Christ. And we all as citizens of the Kingdom of God, whether young or mature, new or old, we all have been given the ministry of reconciliation: reconciling man back to God... "For God so loved the world (not the Church) that He gave His only begotten Son that whosoever believeth in Him should not perish but have everlasting life... John 3:16."

However, if men were to judge the character of God by looking at the state of the Church, it would appear that God is disoriented, not unified, confused and void of any life-changing power.

This is because the Church in most instances do not know who it is nor the power it possesses. As the Church of God and the Lord Jesus, we have mistakenly and incorrectly allowed the world and ungodly men to define who and what the Church is and is not. And as a result of allowing the world to dictate our purpose in society, we have as of late been very ineffective and poor representatives of God's will on earth and His purpose for mankind in-general. By our complacency in declaring righteously and boldly the things of God, we have literally caused the fool to say in His heart "there is no God." Like the religious man Paul speaks about in the second chapter of the epistle of Romans, our hypocritical actions have caused God's name to be blasphemed among the Gentiles. Sadly, many churches in the world today have a form of Godliness but they deny the power thereof.

They say all the right and religious things, but they do not possess any power to effectively change the conditions of their communities for the glory of God.

If you're pastoring a church in a community that is full of crime, drug abuse, unstable families and you haven't made a serious and recognizable change in that community since you've been there, I want you to know that is a terrible and sad commentary of God and His kingdom. Why? Because if you're suppose to be a church you're suppose to be representing and administering the works and fruits of the Kingdom of God.

Therefore anything you do or don't do directly reflects the Kingdom of Heaven and the will of God for mankind.

God has now given the Church the mandate to once again become relative to the problems and concerns of the world and the lives of men. We must begin to express in an effective and powerful manner the will of God on the earth and in the personal lives of men. If this is to be realized we must truly understand who and what the Church is according to the Bible and not according to some denominational creed or some seminaries' theological doctrine. And that is what this book endeavors to do. That being to define the purpose and role of the Church in the world society and the personal lives of individual men. I do not imply by any means that this book is the total and only authority on the Church, only the Bible and God through His Spirit by the person of the Lord Jesus possesses such. But my prayer is that, this book, "The Church," will help you to know God better and understand the purposes of the Church more fully.

Chapter 1

What is the Church?

The word, church, is translated from the Greek word ekklesia, and from the Hebrew word, qara which mean "the called out ones." The first occurrence of the word, church, in the Bible is found in Genesis when Isaac blessed Jacob. "Be a multitude of people." (Genesis 28:3) Although the word was used in the secular world, to the then known world, to the Jews, the word church meant a society that consisted of members who were subject to the law of Jehovah God. The Hebrew word, qahal, is also used when speaking of an assembly, company, congregation or multitude of people. It was Jesus Christ Himself who first applied this term to the Christian society that was soon to be born. "Upon this rock I will build my church." (Matt 16:18) When Jesus told Peter that He would build His church upon the rock, He did not mean that He would build His church upon Peter, who was supposedly the first pope. The Roman Catholic System has erroneously taught that Peter was to be the foundation of the Church, hence he became the first pope.

Peter was never the Pope and Jesus would never build a church on a mortal man who was capable of vacillating, especially on one who was going to deny Him before a maid. Instead, He was going to build His church upon Peter's confession of the deity of Jesus Christ. It was upon the truth that Jesus Christ is the Son of God, the Anointed One, the one and only Savior of the world, that the church would be built. If Jesus Christ was not God and the only Savior of man, the universal Church falls to the ground. Jesus was going to build His church upon a rock. A rock denotes a foundation that is strong and lasting. Jesus will not build His church on sand that cannot carry the weight of the building when the winds and storm arise. But the foundation of the Church will be upon the rock that will not sink under the heaviest attack of the spiritual world. The gates of hell, which will attempt to destroy it, will not prevail against it, for the Church is founded upon the rock.

A rock is not on the same level with the world, so is the Church of Jesus Christ. It will stand tall and strong above the world. The world will look up to it as a refuge. Life is safer and richer because of the Church. The influence of the Church in the world is what has stopped the flood of moral decay from divulging the world. In the world, the Church stands as the light that shines in darkness.

Unfortunately, many people do not respect and recognize the Church as they should because they do not know what the Church is in actuality.

Countless professing believers do not have an understanding of the meaning of "church," never mind the nonbeliever. America thinks that her school system does not need the Church. The Bible is no longer respected and taught in our public schools. Prayer has become taboo. Why should the government be alarmed at the rate sin is escalating? The Ten Commandments that the Church stands for are being rejected. Children are losing respect for their parent. Teenagers talk of practicing safe sex. Teenage suicide is on the increase. Guns and violence have found their way into the classrooms.

The moral fiber is weak. The truth that the Church preaches is being neglected to the destruction of the children. The truth upon which the Church is founded is the hope for the future. When the Church is taken away, there is no more light to shine in the darkness of moral decay.

The Church has the answer to the world's problems, for it is the mouthpiece of God. The oracles of God have been committed to the Church. Politicians do not have the answer to the problems we face today. The Church has the answers, for the true Church proclaims that Jesus Christ is the solution. There can be no peace without the Prince of Peace.

If the Church were recognized and respected there would be less violence and problems. It bears repeating that many people do not know what the Church is in actuality. They are confusing the

Church with religion. I do not want your religion, and I hope you do not want mine. You can go to hell with your religion. It is not religion that saves, but your relationship with Jesus Christ.

You must be part of the universal Church, the called out ones. These are the people who have made Jesus as their Lord, they have forsaken the world, and joined the Church of Jesus Christ.

Jesus Christ is the builder of the Church. "I will build my church" He said. He did not say your church. The Church belongs to Jesus Christ. It is His. He is the Builder and Maker of it. Abraham never found the city whose Maker and Builder was God. He saw it with the eyes of faith, but he was never to be part of it. The city, whose Builder and Maker is God, is the Church.

The Church is the connection of the world to God. I am not talking of the building. I am talking of the called out-ones whose foundation is based upon the deity of Jesus Christ; and whose message is centered on the death, burial and resurrection of Jesus Christ.

The Church is the visible manifestation of Jesus Christ. We bear His image. The earth may belong to the Lord, but the Church is the called out-ones that reflect the glory of Jesus Christ. The commission of going into the world to preach the gospel of Jesus Christ has been given to the Church. The message of the Church, based upon the truth of the Gospel is what saves.

Like her Builder, the Church is supernatural. Conversions of the most morally depraved man into a saint points to the supernatural nature of the Church of Jesus Christ. She has stood the testings of time. But like a rock, she has stood firm and strong amidst the turbulence that has assayed to drown her. Persecution has not destroyed her, instead it has made her strong and vibrant. The martyrs have gone to the lion's dens with the peace of God that passes all understanding. This supernatural peace amidst tribulation has guarded her.

The main reason you are alive is to preserve the Church of Jesus Christ, which is His body. If the Church is not preserved, corruption will destroy the nation, for the Church is the salt of the earth. You are not of the world, although you live in it. Jesus Christ pointed out that He did not pray that the Father would take the Church out of the world prematurely, but that He should keep them from the evil one. (John 17:15)

You are not of the world. Do not allow the world to infect or defile you. Instead, take the light of the Word of God and let it shine in this world of darkness and moral failure. Let your light so shine when people see you, they will ask you the secret to your life.

The Church, like her Spiritual Head, is the light of the world. Things are getting so bad. Every other thing has failed. Education has not provided us with answer to the human need. Technology and politics too have failed. The rich and the famous have discovered the deceitfulness of sin. After gaining money and fame, they have come to the conclusion that these do not provide inner satis-faction. Fulfillment, my friend is not found in money. It is not found in materialism. It does not reside in fame.

The United Nations has no answer for the world's problem. They cannot fight principalities and powers. The American army cannot fight princi-palities and powers. These powers are behind abortion, homosexuality, lesbianism, drugs, vio-lence and so on. Legislation is not good enough. You may have all that life has to offer, yet you may remain empty inside. Satisfaction is found only in Jesus Christ. If only the church people would live like they should, peoples' lives would be touched and changed. If they would see the beauty of the Lord in you, they would hold on to your skirt and say, "Where are you going?" When they learn of the secret of your success, they will say, "I will go with you. Take me with you." You may then lead them to the saving knowledge of God through Jesus Christ.

Some ministers talk about their ministry all day long. God is not building your ministry. He is not concerned about your church. He is concerned, primarily about His church. If the purpose of your ministry or church is to build up the universal Church of God, God will help you. But if you use your ministry or church to build only your ego, God is not interested, and you may even end up with it in hell if you don't live right or you do not belong in the universal Church. You cannot impress God with your ministry. God is interested foremost in His church. The universal Church is the apple of God's eye. Be careful how you treat the called-out ones. They are very precious in His sight. If you are living for anything else, you are missing it. Do you pray, "Thy Kingdom come?" Or is your prayer centered around getting a job, buying a good car and living in a nice home? We are to seek first, the kingdom before material things. (Matt 6:33) You are supposed to pray for the kingdom of God. We are to pray that the kingdom of Christ would come. The kingdom of God which is simply another name for the kingdom of Heaven, is to be our constant focus.

When Jesus founded His church, after the resurrection, it was an aspect of the operation of the kingdom of God. The Kingdom of God talks of the reign of God. Ever since Adam disobeyed God, and sold out to the devil, it has been God's intention, to regain the world to Himself. It was first to begin in the hearts of the called out-ones - the Church. Hence, when Jesus and John the Baptist began their public ministry, they spoke of the coming of the Kingdom which was near because, the Church was soon to be inaugurated by Christ, where God would reign.

The Church is therefore a partial manifestation of the Kingdom of God. Yet, there is to be another aspect of the Kingdom that we must yearn for, when God's reign will be recognized upon earth.

In the meantime, we must pray for the expansion of God's kingdom in the heart of men. We must not only pray for the kingdom, we must also preach it. The Lord has given His church the keys of the kingdom. The keys denote authority. We have power with God. He has given us authority to bind and to loose, to uproot and to tear down. (Matt 16:19)

The Church must stand up to her responsibility. We must carry the torch to the world that gropes in darkness. We must be bearers of peace to a chaotic world that is being torn apart by the evils of this present age.

We have the answer to the problems the world is facing. We hold the keys of the kingdom of God. With it, let us open the hearts of men to the truth of the Gospel upon which we are founded. The truth is embedded in the reality that Jesus is indeed the Son of God, the Savior that came into the world to bear away the sin of the world. And in receiving this truth, people can also become part of the universal Body of Jesus Christ.

Chapter 2

The Origin and Election of the Church

The Church was not founded on the day of Pentecost as some suggest. It had already been in existence before Pentecost. When Mary saw Jesus on the resurrection morning, He told her, "Touch me not, for I am not yet ascended to my Father, but go to my brethren, and say unto them, I ascend unto my Father and your Father and to my God and your God." (John 20:17) While Mary went to proclaim the good news of the resurrected Lord, Jesus ascended to heaven to present Himself to the Father. O what glorious time this must have been in heaven! What song must have been on the lips of the angels!

The salvation of the human race had been completed. The Son of God had finished the work that the Father had given Him. He had not shirked from death for He was born to die for the penalty of our sin. And He did die. Now He had gone back to heaven and His Father had accepted the ultimate sacrifice.

The Father of Jesus Christ could now become the Father of the Church that was soon to be inaugurated, later on in the day. His God had to become her God as well, for the Church was to now be the body of Jesus Christ. Jesus came back to the earth once again the same day. By now it was evening.

Think about it. Jesus went back to heaven physically, and was back in the evening! "Then the same day at evening, being the first day of the week, when the doors were shut where the disciples were assembled for fear of the Jews, came Jesus and stood in the midst,, and saith unto them, Peace be unto you." (John 20:19) Jesus then proceeded to show them His hand and His feet that it was Him and not someone else.

Next he commissioned them to go and preach the gospel, at which time He breathed into the disciples and said, "Receive ye the Holy Ghost." This was not the Spirit Baptism but the Spiritual New Birth. This was when the disciples became born again. They could not have been born again without the death and the resurrection of Jesus Christ. They were born again of the Spirit on the evening of Resurrection Day.

On the day of Pentecost, the Holy Spirit descended, not to give new life to the disciples. He did not descend to start the Church. The disciples had received new life on Resurrection Day. The Church had been formed. The reason for the descent of the Holy Spirit was to endue the weak born-again disciples with power just like their Lord.

It is only in Jesus Christ that the breath of life can be imparted. Eternal life is found only in Jesus Christ. There is no other foundation. No other way, by which life can be imparted, except as through Jesus Christ. This new birth was experienced on the evening of Resurrection Day. Now the disciples could understand Jesus.

When Jesus used to tell them about the things of God they could not understand what He was saying. Once Jesus told them to beware of the leaven of Pharisees, which was hypocrisy, but the disciples failed to recognize what the leaven was. They took it to be the physical yeast. Later after His resurrection, Jesus had a teaching session with two of His disciples who were on their way to Emmaus. How they were capable of understanding, because now they were born again.

The Bible says that He opened their understanding that they might understand the scriptures. Before, they could not understand the scriptures, but now, after the resurrection, their understanding could be enlightened. The unbeliever is incapable of understanding the Bible. (1 Cor. 2:14) They may know it in their head, but they cannot understand it with their spirit. That is why, Christianity is not a set of rules. It is not a religion. It is a living relationship with Jesus Christ. No one had the eternal life in the Old Testament. Eternal life is in the Son. The Jews in the Old Testament knew the Father, but they did not know the Son.

You must know both the Father and the Son to have eternal life. "And this is eternal life, that they might know thee, the only true God and Jesus Christ whom thou hast sent." (John 17:3)

Judaism only knows of the Father, hence, there is no eternal life in it. Only Christianity has life in it, for eternal life is in the Son. "For God so loved the world, that he gave his only begotten son, that whosoever believeth in Him should not perish but have everlasting life." (John 3:16) You must believe in the Son to have everlasting life.

The other religions of the world do not have life in them for they do not have the Son. These religions may be morally upright. They may have good codes of conduct. The Islam religion calls God Allah. But they only know Him by name only. Because they do not have the Son, they cannot have eternal life, and therefore cannot relate to God. The election of the Church, although the Church was inaugurated on Resurrection Day, her election was however of an earlier date. The election of the Church and Jews were effected on different dates. God had elected the Church before the foundation of the world or before the beginning of time. It was because the first Adam sinned that God chose Abraham to be the father of the nation of Israel through whom He would temporarily reveal Himself. If the original people had not messed up, He would not have had to choose another set of people.

The Jews were to be God's special people, as a nation, a prototype of the eternal Church, until the fullness of time comes, when God's eternal purpose will be revealed. His eternal plan was the Church. He had chosen the Church, long before Abraham was born. It has existed in His thought. It was not something that He woke up one day and decided to effect. God always has a plan about everything He does. He has a counsel within Him before He does anything. He is a God of order.

In the beginning, God said, "Let us make man..." When Jesus came into the world, He said, "I will build my church." Now put the two statements together and you get the purpose of God for making man. Let us make man to build the Church. God's original plan for making man was to build His church.

The Church is therefore not just two thousand years old. It is much older than that. The Church was chosen before the world began. "Who hath saved us, and called us with an holy calling, not according to our works, but according to his own purpose and grace, which was given us in Christ Jesus before the world began, But is now made manifest by the appearing of our Savior Jesus Christ, who hath abolished death and hath brought life and immortality to light through the gospel." (2 Tim 1:9-10)

So we see that God had already elected the Church before the foundation of the world, before time began. But the Church was made manifest two thousand years ago when Jesus died and rose from the dead. Jesus, as the Lamb of God had been slain before the foundation of the world. It was in the thought of God that Jesus would come and form a group of "called out ones".

When Adam sinned, God was not taken by surprise. He was not confused. He did not panic because He had made a provision for it. He knew that Adam would fall, and so He had provided the salvation of man in the person of Jesus Christ. Or it can be said, that the visible manifestation of the Church took place on the resurrection, but the election had already taken place before time began. The Bible says that the first man is earthly. The second man is spiritual. As we are born of the image of the earthly man, so must we be born in the image of the heavenly man. It was God who decided that the spiritual man must be the second to come. That is why we are not to be condemned by the failure in the garden because that is not the end. The same man who failed in the garden is going to bounce back and become spiritual in the end. Praise God!

The Church is, therefore, not a human creation. It is God Himself who elected her. Her origin before the foundation of the world is traced to God. The Church is, thus, dependent on Jesus Christ, for He is the Builder, the One who reared it. He therefore supports it and fights for it. Nothing can destroy it for its origin is in God. No weapon of the enemy, be it physical enemy of spiritual enemy, that is formed against her shall avail. The Church is in Jesus Christ, and Jesus Christ is in God. The Church of Jesus Christ is there safe and secure. She is strong like her Savior, for her origin and continual existence is in Jesus Christ.

I am not talking about a building. I am not talking about a denomination. God is not a segregationist. He is not a Baptist, or a Methodist, neither is He any of the other denominations, either denominational or independent. God is not a Republican, by the way. He is neither a Democrat. The Church that God recognizes is the invisible universal Church, composed of those who have received eternal life in His Son Jesus Christ.

Chapter 3

The Church - An Organism

The Church of Jesus Christ is an organism. An organism is a living entity. The Church therefore has life. It is pulsating with the life of God. Hence, the Bible compares the Church to a body. The Church is not primarily an organization. An organization can remove and replace some part and still be intact. But if you remove a part from a body, like an eye, foot, or ears, they cannot be replaced. The image of the body will be destroyed. You cannot replace these members with false ones. If you do, the body is still not whole.

The church government may be an organization, but the living men and women in it form the organism. The Church is therefore the body of Christ with various members. Each part is important. The body of Christ is an organism. You cannot hurt a member of the body and not deface the whole body. Be careful how you treat your fellow brothers and sisters. Be careful what you tell them and how you tell them. As a living organism, there will be friction, and that means there would be hurt. You cannot say that each time you get hurt in a church you are going to leave. You will experience the same hurt elsewhere. This is why the role of the pastor is so important.

The Pastor's Role

The pastor is the local head, just like Christ is the spiritual and the universal Head of the Church. The pope is not the head, but the pastor. There is no mention of any pope in the Bible. The pastor is responsible for the spiritual vitality of the Church.

When the Lord was going to send a message to earth through John when he was on the land of Patmos, it was not to the apostle or member of the Church that the message was sent. It was sent to the angel. For example, in sending a message to Ephesus, Jesus said, "Unto the angel of the church of Ephesus, write these things....." (Rev 2:1)

The angel that was addressed here was not the angel of heaven, else, there would be no need to send a message to them on earth since they reside in heaven. Instead, the angel here stood for the pastor of the named church. Why? Because, the pastor is the head of the church. The pastor is the main person.

The five-fold office has been given the responsibility to see to the welfare of the sheep. No church can operate without the pastor, just like no body can operate without the head. The body will not be able to coordinate at all. This is the importance of the office of the pastor. You must acknowledge who your local head is, and make a concrete decision to follow him/her. This way, you will lessen the pastor's load. The office of the apostle God has given the church other five-fold ministers or ascensions gifts as well. (Eph. 4:11) They form the hand of God over His church.

The apostle represents the thumb because this person is in a better position to touch others. The apostle is the sent out one. They have extraordinary charisma to found churches, and to produce mighty works. It is the foremost office, not in the local church but in the universal church. They tell you what to do with authority.

Paul was one of the most important apostles in the early church in that he wrote 13-14 of the 28 books which comprise the New Testament. He also made reference to Andronicus and Junia being "... of note among the apostles." (Rom 16:7). They possibly were husband and wife according to recent discoveries of earlier manuscripts.

The Office of the Prophet

The prophet is the index finger. They point at you and they are gone. They are apt in expounding the Scriptures with prophetic insights. It is not necessarily what they learn in Bible school, but they have an unusual level of insight given by the Holy Spirit. They bring prophetic correction and direction in addition to edification and encouragement. This is one of the main distinguishing characteristics of the office of prophet as opposed to the "gift of prophecy."

One operating in the gift of prophecy does not have the authority or the anointing to bring words of correction and direction to the pastor or the congregation. Barnabas was an example of the New Testament prophet. The prophets do not only forth-tell from God, they also foretell. They can predict things to come, or see something about people supernaturally.

Agabus prophesied about the impending danger that faced Paul in Jerusalem. Anna, the prophet-ess, spoke prophetically of the redemption of our Lord, giving thanks upon presentation of baby Jesus by Joseph and Mary at the temple. It is noted that Anna's life was one of serving God with prayers and fasting, and she did not depart from the local temple. (Luke 2:37)

The Office of the Evangelist

The evangelist is the one with an unusual bur-den for souls representing the middle finger. As the longest finger, they reach to the ends of the earth with the gospel of Jesus Christ. Their concern for the souls leads them to go from place to place, endeavoring to win souls for Christ.

Their waking thought and their sleeping thoughts are strategies on how to win souls. The true evan-gelists are not out to promote their names or their ministries. Their primary concern is to see that souls are brought to the saving knowledge of Jesus Christ. Every Christian is called to be a soul winner. So, do not push the responsibility of winning souls to the evangelists alone.

However, the zeal of the evangelist separates this person from the church in terms of his or her strong desire to win souls for Christ. Philip was a true evangelist. One cannot but notice his zeal for souls. After igniting revival fires in Samaria, the Spirit carried him to a desert where he led the first African to Christ. Stephen (Acts 6:8-9; 7:2-53) demonstrates the office of an evangelist.

The Office of the Pastor

The pastor is the fourth finger, the finger that wears the wedding ring. This person is married to the church. The apostle might have founded the church, and the evangelist might have brought in souls, but the task of feeding the sheep, tending to their needs, applying the balm to the wound, making them lie down in green pastures, warding off the enemies and willingness to lay down ones life for the local church is given to the pastor. He/she is the one who knows them like no other. The pastor has spent time with them and knows what the members are doing.

When they speak, the pastor knows where they are coming from. He knows their spiritual, social, emotional and economic backgrounds and can relate to them at their levels. The other offices may come and go, but the pastor remains. He may leave for awhile, but his position is one of constant companionship. He decides who he allows to minister on the pulpit, and he alone should inflict discipline where necessary. He is the best one qualified to do so, and not members of the church.

The Office of the Teacher

The teacher represents the smallest finger. This is the one who breaks down the Word of God so that even a little child can understand. He/she puts in an orderly manner, the teachings of the Bible, and relates them to the issues of life. The teacher is gifted to be able to divide the word of truth, pointing out the different emphasis the Bible places on different topics. He is constantly studying the Word. It is an awesome responsibility, to teach not only the whole counsel of God, but to teach them in a way as to be comprehensible to one's hearers.

The Pivotal Office

The pivotal office upon which the local church turns is that of the pastor. He is the head of the local church. When the devil wants to destroy the local church, his primary target is the pastor. "... smite the shepherd, and the sheep will scatter ..." (Zec 13:7) That is why the members must pray daily for the pastor. He is in a critical post. The devil knows that if he could destroy the pastor, the local church is destroyed.

When God communicates the vision, it is to the pastor of the church with whom He communicates.

You must obey the head. When God communicates to your pastor about an issue, it is not in your place to begin to criticize and murmur. God speaks to the head about the direction of the church, not the hands or the feet.

The head sends a message to the feet to take the body to a certain place, and the feet obey. When the pastor stands up to give a vision, given him by the Lord, it is not for your endorsement. It is not for you to agree, but to obey. There is a gross lack of discipline in the local church today. People are trying to infiltrate the church with the insubordinate attitude they have in the world. In the church, it is Christ Jesus who has set these offices. The pastor is your local head, and you should obey and respect him.

Restoration and Function of Five-Fold Ministers

It is imperative that the authority of this office along with the corresponding responsibility be fully understood by all. The pastor must be one whom has attained a level of maturity which will enable him or her to carry the weight of this office with grace and humility. Then the people willingly, will submit just as a wife will to a husband who loves her as Christ loved the church. (Eph 5:25) Once this is accomplished in the hearts of all concerned then the full restoration at the church on earth will be attained.

All five-fold ministers must submit to the final authority of the Senior Pastor to keep the order of headship and God's divine vision for that local assembly. Some important advantages to recognizing and encouraging the functioning of these ministry offices within the local body is that:

(1) the life of the Senior Pastor will be lengthened, for now the burden need not be shouldered totally alone by the pastor.

(2) The pastor may expect a higher level of commitment and service from those who are fully installed in their ascension offices to the fulfillment of the vision that God has spoken to the Senior. Pastor's heart.

(3) Where the pastor is not particularly gifted, allow the one(s) who are gifted to flow. If the pastor is a preacher but not a teacher, then allow the ones who stand in the office of Teacher to conduct the Bible Study and give the teaching messages. As the people see the unity and power they will begin to realize in a way that "can not be taught but must be caught" that there is only one Holy Spirit. They will begin to understand that God has spread His anointing throughout His people and it has not been bestowed on only one person, namely the Senior Pastor.

(4) Also, this will bring the local church closer to the first century model of church government. This was one of the keys to why the Church was a force to be reckoned with in the world at that time. The saints were being perfected by God's hand for the work of the ministry.

The Senior Pastor must pray for these ministry offices to be raised up or sent to his fellowship. God will grant discernment so that he/she should be joined with the ones revealed to themselves. Most importantly, the apostle and the prophet must be encouraged to speak into the lives of the leadership and pastorate. This will insure that divine direction and foresight are being laid into the foundation of the local church and the universal Church. (Eph 2:20)

There are some "things" which must be restored and until such time as they are "... Jesus Christ, which before was preached unto you: whom the heaven must receive until the times of restitution of all things; which God hath spoken by the mouth of all his holy prophets since the world began." (Acts 3:20-21)

Chapter 4

The Restoration of the Church

"The sun shall be turned into darkness, and the moon into blood, before the great and notable day of the Lord." (Acts 2:20) When revival broke out in the church in the 1800's, God began to restore His church with a greater intensity. He is restoring to the church all that was lost down the ages. The notable day of the Lord is fast approaching, but the church has to be willing to change. The danger lies in the fact that when God begins to restore, and you are not sensitive to His approach, you may be left behind. If God works against the traditions of your local church, and you refuse to give them up, watch out, you may be bypassed! But the work of restoration will march on. God is the Builder of His church, and He may do as He pleases. Like Israel in the wilderness, you have to follow the cloud of the working of God.

Martin Luther was a Roman Catholic who lived under the superstitious mood that prevailed in the church of his times. He had been taught lies upon lies. He was told that the way to heaven was through penitence and paying money to the church. He believed the lie. He tried to be holy and had to go for confession and penance ever so often. One day, the priest that was used to hearing his confession of trivial sins told him to go commit a more serious sin before coming to confession.

Martin wondered about a God who was so difficult to please. But, thank God, as clergy, he had access to the Bible. He was studying the Epistle to the Romans, when he came across the words, "The just shall live by faith." Scales fell from his eyes, as He met the God who justifies through faith and faith alone in the atoning death of Jesus Christ.

The more Luther searched the Scriptures, the more He became convinced that justification came through faith and faith alone, without the other works prescribed by the Roman Catholic system, such as penitence and good works. Martin began to share his new found faith. It was not long, before the Roman Catholic System persecuted him because justification by faith alone did not square with their teaching of the Bible.

Luther was adamant and insisted on this newfound truth, which was really not new, but was rediscovered. The Roman Catholic system had covered it under the rubles of her traditional teaching but it took a simple, truth-loving person like Martin to rediscover this truth. Luther maintained that only the Scriptures must be taught and obeyed.

The Roman Catholic church objected. They wanted to hold on to their tradition. But Luther's Sola Scriptura (Scriptures alone) earned him persecution from his church, and ultimately expulsion from the false system, but not from the invisible true Church of God. The Protestant church was thus born. God was overlooking the affairs of His church. The gates of hell will not prevail against it. God continues to move at the most critical points in the history of the church. Many men and women could be cited in the pages of the Church history who dared defy the Roman Catholic System to stand on the Scriptures alone as the rule of doctrine and life-style. God again is moving by His Spirit, in the Church. He is preparing leaders who will lead the people right. Leaders who are trained and have prepared themselves. Without a leader, people will stray into heresy and false dogma.

In the early church, when God was moving in a supernatural way, conversion to Christianity was a common place. Miracles, healings and supernatural acts accompanied these conversions. Churches were springing from every quarter at an amazing rate. The Jews, the Africans, the Greeks and so on were flooding the universal, true Church of God.

But leadership was rare. There were few teachers and pastors to handle these churches. There were many babies, but few fathers, many disciples, but few leaders. It was not before long that false teachings began to creep into the churches. The Jewish Christians insisted that the Church should be circumcised. Paul had a rough time setting the doctrines straight. As a matter of fact, most of the epistles written by Paul are refutations of the many doctrines that had crept into the church. The epistle of Galatians refuted the doctrine of Judaism as incumbent on the Church.

The epistle to the Colossians was a rebuttal of the Greek gnostic tendencies that denied the divine and the human side of Jesus Christ and claim a special access to a kind of knowledge outside of Jesus Christ. The epistle to the Corinthian, discusses the charismata or the gifts of the Holy Spirit, which was causing confusion in the church due to inappropriateness on the part some of members.

John the Beloved, wrote his first epistle as a defense of the humanity of Jesus Christ. Thank God for these able ministers of the first century who were capable of leading the Church right through persecution under the power of the Holy Spirit! Today, leaders are needed to handle the restoration God is bringing into His church. These leaders must be ready to assume their post when called upon. They must be filled with the Holy Spirit, and be saturated in the written Word of God. They must not turn from it, to the right or to the left. They must be ready to roll away the tradition that does not agree with the Word. They must be humble in order to flow with the Holy Spirit in these last days. Democracy versus Theocracy, God is the builder and the sustainer of His church. He does not depend on any one person or denomination to move. He moves irrespective of what the deacons or elders of those dead churches say. The man of God does not have to have the approval of these leaders of dead churches to move. If Martin Luther had waited for Pope Leo VIII to approve the justification by faith, he would have been lost.

Or, if William Seymor had listened to the anti-pentecost of his day to launch the greatest revival since reformation, God would probably have by-passed him and used someone else. I do not advocate the lone-ranger syndrome in which the individual does not receive any advice from God-fearing men and women who know and serve God.

However, I reject the idea of receiving counsel from a religious committee of men and women who are in spiritual darkness and do not recognize the move of God. I once visited the home of a dear pastor in Haiti. He had an interesting inscription on his wall which caught my eye. It read, "For God so loved the world, that He did not send a committee." How true the message! Some churches are ruled by deacons who make up the committee.

These deacons are given the power to vote for or against the pastor. They hire him and they fire him. They are the rulers of the church. And often, they are not spiritual people. Some of them do not even know the Lord. Their Bible is the tradition of men. But the office of the deacon in the New Testament is different.

The word "deacon" is a transliteration of the Greek word diakonos which means "a waiter, attendant, or servant." The office came into being, when there was murmuring in the church because the Grecian widows were neglected in food distribution. The apostles asked the church to choose men of spiritual maturity who would look into these practical matters, in order to free the hands of the apostles for prayer and teaching of the Word. (Acts 6:1-4)

The office of the deacon was not created to lord it over the pastor. Deacons are supposed to be subject to their local head, who is the pastor. Because of the unbiblical power given to this committee of deacons, a lot of pastors have lost their vision. They have become a puppet in the hands of these people. They are bound from preaching the uncompromised Word of God because they might step on some deacon's foot.

The pastor, as the local head must hear from God, and do what God tells him to do. When God gives a vision, it is usually to a person, and He then supplies him with people who will carry out the vision. The vision is not given to the people but to the individual. That is why you have no business attending a church if you can not embrace the vision of the pastor. Get out, and look for somewhere else and find a pastor you may serve in implementing God's vision. When God was going to send Jesus Christ to the world, He did not consult those stiff-neck so called church deacons and elders to get their vote. Had He done so, they would have continued to argue and vote about the pros and cons of the proposal while precious souls went to a Christ-less eternity. But, thank God, that is not what the Bible says. God did not send a committee. He did not even send a host of angels. He sent a man, with a vision. He sent Jesus Christ, "... His only begotten Son, so that, anyone who believes in Him should not perish, but have everlasting life." (John 3:16) When God wants to do something, He calls a man or a woman to accomplish a mission for Him. They do not have to ask for permission from these spiritually-insensitive elders. When Jesus came to Jerusalem, He did not go to the Sanhedrin to get their permission to carry out the vision God had given Him. He did not try to be in their good graces. He knew the vision that God had given to Him, and He was determined to carry it out, irrespective of what the so-called spiritual leaders said.

He told them one day, that He did whatever He saw His Father do. (John 5:19) You too, must hear from God. You must know what God has told you to do. You must be convinced beyond every doubt of the mission God has called you to do. Then do it. You do not need permission from some deacon to do it. "And the heavens departed as a scroll when it is rolled together; and every mountain and island were moved out to their places." (Revelation 6:14) The heaven departed as a scroll when it is rolled together. The mountain, and the island will move out of their places. When God visits His church with a revival, you must roll up the scroll to give way to new scrolls that are approaching. You must roll up your traditional beliefs and creeds that have no place in the Bible.

The Methodist, the Baptists, the Episcopalian, the Pentecostal must all roll up their old beliefs and traditional teachings. If they don't they will be left behind in the next revival when the church is marching on in triumph. When God moves, He wants us to get ready for His move and discern what He is saying. Everyone who has ears should hear what God is saying to the church.

Tradition

The church must be willing to roll over the tradition of the elders that oppose the Scriptures. No where is it written that the committee must vote before an action is taken. The church is not a democratic rule, but a theocratic rule. The church is not ruled by the vote of its members. The church belongs, first and foremost to God. He is the Builder and He decides what He wants for His church. The church polity should therefore be theocratic. Moses found himself in this web of denominational voting. There were 12 voters. God had promised the children of Israel that He would given them the land of Canaan. So, Moses sent 12 spies, one from each tribe, to spy the land.

When they got to the land, they saw big men of stature, that they looked like dwarfs in comparison to them. They became so afraid, they abandoned the idea of possessing the land. But God had promised them that He would give them the land as their possession. The word was supposed to have generated faith in their hearts. The children of God are supposed to walk by faith, and not by sight.

The twelve spies came back each with a report. Ten of them said they could not take the land, because the inhabitants were giants. But two came with a different report. Joshua and Caleb saw, not the giants, but the power of their God. Their report was that they could take the land. They sided with God.

The vote was ten against two. The scale was in favor of men of unbelief. The minority was in the will of God, while the majority voice was the will of the devil. That is the havoc that voting usually brings. But Moses should have known better. God had told him that He had given them the land for their possession. Hence, Moses was not able to enter the promised land. He listened to the voice of the people, instead of the voice of God. In the church, democracy should not prevail. The rule by the people for the people is not tenable in the church of God. The only tenable form of government is theocracy, the rule of God and God alone. The church must be ready for the move of God. We must cast aside the writ of religiosity and traditional teaching that has clogged the wheel of spiritual revival.

We must be sensitive to the move of God that is beginning to descend on the church for the final time before the notable day of the Lord. We must roll away the scrolls to give room to the move of God. Are you ready? During a meeting in my old church, the board announced the pregnancy of an unmarried sister. They were contemplating what measure of disciplinary action was to be given to her. One member suggested that she should be expelled. The red book, stated that she was to be put out of the church. But what does the Bible say? The following day, I went to see the pregnant young woman. I did not confront her with her sins. I simply gave her $100.00 to go and see a doctor. I asked her to report to me as soon as possible when the baby was due. I assured her I was praying for her. I also told her that I knew she had repented of this grievous sin and had received God's forgiveness. Man may continue to judge you and hold it against you, but God has forgiven. The following day, with tears in her eyes, she told me the date the baby was expected. I told her to be in church for communion the following Sunday. Before the communion was served, I invited her to the front, before the whole congregation. I went on to tell the church that she was pregnant out of wedlock.

In accordance to the red book, she was to be excommunicated. She did not have the right to the Holy Communion we were all about to partake of. She must first go on probation. That was the rule of the red book. But she has repented of her sins. I then asked the church for a verdict on her. If she had repented and received forgiveness from God, should she have to wait for nine months after the baby was born before she could be restored? I placed my hand on her stomach and asked the congregation if the baby was a sin in and of itself. At least, she kept the baby and did not abort it like others would have done. Therefore, I believe she needed the communion more than any of us. This young woman was not rebellious. She did not have a nonchalant attitude about what she had done. Must she be pressured to abort the baby in order to remove some heat laid on her by the church? Or must she be encouraged that it was not the end of the world, and that God still loved her anyhow. She did not have to sit at the back of the church to invoke judgmental look of the members of the congregation. The young woman received the love the church gave to her. Now she is a married woman and the boy is a teenager now. He is saved and filled with the Holy Spirit. They both still belong to the church. But who knows what might have happened had I followed the rule of the red book instead of the Bible.

The Jews brought a woman who had been caught in the act of adultery to Jesus. Incidentally, the man was not brought along with her. They wanted to go according to the book that she must be stoned. But Jesus saw the inside of this woman. He saw the potential that lay buried in her. He saw a woman in spiritual need, not of judgment but of forgiveness.

He did not come into the world to judge the world but to save the world. Instead of commanding her to be stoned, He spared her life and gave her a second chance. He then told her to go and sin no more.

Can you imagine the gratitude that gripped this woman's heart. She went away justified, forgiven and emotionally healed. This was not a luxury her self-righteous and religious opponents enjoyed. She had been given a new opportunity. That is the business we should be in as Christians. We are in the business of reconciliation. We are not condoning sin, but we must be careful to be led by the Spirit of God in delicate issues such as this. The church of today must position herself ready for the restoration that God is bringing to the church. We must be willing to set aside the unbiblical traditional teachings that have plagued us these many years. Jesus told the religious leaders of His day to roll away the traditions of men which hindered them from obeying the Word of God. We have to roll away the scrolls of religious teaching that have been passed from generation to generation.

Racism

The church of today has to roll up the scrolls of prejudice that were written about the Black people. The myth that the Black race was cursed must be dispelled. On the contrary, the first man from which all mankind came from was black. The geographical location of Eden dictates the ethnicity of Adam. (Gen 2:11-14) If the Black man is under a curse, so is all of mankind; for all other races came from this first man. A genetic product is never better than its source of origin. There is archeological evidence for the fact that the first man was black. The skull of the most ancient man was found in the country of Ethiopia on the continent of Africa and it was a Black man's skull. There was a cover story about this finding in U.S. News and World Report on September 16, 1991. There has never been and it will never be a time when God will forsake or cursed the Black race.

Many white brethren lack respect for their Black brethren. They look down on Blacks and other races and assume an air of superiority. This attitude of pride, ignorance and immaturity must be eradicated in the Body of Christ. The early church of Antioch respected the Black leadership. When Paul and Barnabas were going to be sent out as missionaries, the leaders of the church, which included some Blacks, laid hands on Paul and his companion. (Acts 13-13)

Today, some churches do not welcome or truly accept Blacks in there congregation, talk less of submitting to their authority. Yet, the greatest apostle needed the prayer of these Black leaders. The church needs to go back to the basics and realize that God is not color blind of races; but colorfully appreciative of different races and equally inclusive of all creeds in His plan to evangelize the world to Christ.

At the turn of the century, when the church would not allow Blacks to worship with them, God decided to bypass them and start a revival, headed by a Black man on Azusa Street in Los Angeles, California. It is one of the greatest revivals in the Church. We are still feeling its impact to the present time.

Ministers all over the world came to Azusa street, to attend the service pastored by a Black man, to receive the baptism of the Holy Spirit with the evidence of speaking in tongues. For three whole years, meetings continued three times a day. Miracles were wrought. Racial prejudice was minimal at the worst.

These great ministers in their respective churches bowed down before this simple uneducated Black man to receive prayers. They saw the cloud of glory, and they moved with it. They received their blessing. Today, the church must be willing to acknowledge that God is raising up different races, that have been despised and trodden down. God is moving among Blacks and many other races.

By the year 2,000 it is has projected that Africa will be the most Christianized continent in the world. God is raising Black churches and great men. Africa has the second largest church in the world, Deeper Life Church in Lagos, Nigeria, with over 65,000 members.

God is raising great leaders from Africa, from America and the Islands. Great black leaders are emerging and assuming leadership just like in the church of Antioch. But some white American and European theologians have propagated the lie that when Noah, a Black man, cursed Canaan, He was cursing all peoples of African descent. This lie, which was born from racial prejudice of some in the church has kept the Black race in chains of bondage to so called biblically based-God and ordained inferiority. (Gen 9:25) If a person thinks that they are under a curse, they will behave like they are under a curse. As a man thinketh in his heart so is he. (Prov 23:7)

The white brethren must be wiling to accept the fact that Black people and other races also have spiritual authority which they should be able to wield without prejudice. They must accept that God has equally called Blacks and other races to be apostles, prophets, evangelist, pastors and teachers. God is not a repector of persons and He will not support overt racism or quiet-sneaky racism. Often when racism is confronted, many claim in words, to avoid the issues, that "we are all one in Christ and members of the Body of Christ." These responses sound great, but many times they fail to truly reflect the thoughts, intents and actions of the people being confronted.

It is time that the church recognized the truth and roll up the scroll of racial prejudice, superiority complex and plain ignorance and endeavor to treat every race has a equal creation of God.

Chapter 5

The Battle Against Sin - The First War

The weapon of this battle is not physical, for it is not a human weapon. Human weapons are designed for human warfare. The physical can fight with the physical. But the weapon that the church of God will need must commensurate with the warfare that is being waged. It is a spiritual warfare. Paul wrote to the Corinthians the nature of the Christian warfare. It is a spiritual warfare, and we have within our reach, spiritual weapons. We must know about these weapons in order to be able to appropriate them.

No warfare is pleasant. By its very nature, in warfare, suffering is imminent. There must be casualties. There must be agony and anguish and sorrow. But, victory is certain if we use these weapons. There are three battles that we must engage in. I call them, the three world wars.

First War

The first war now rages within you. Paul described it in the seventh chapter of Romans, verse 2: "But I see another law in my members, warring

against the law of my mind, and bringing me into
captivity to the law of sin which is in my members."
Paul lamented over the war that was raging within
him. One part of him wanted to live a certain way.
This part delighted in the law of God. It wanted to
please God and carry out the commandments of
God to perfection. It assented to the fact that the
law of God was good, and perfect and holy. But
there was another part of him that was against the
law of God. That part was the sin in his flesh.
Notice that Paul did not attribute the enemy at this
time to the devil. He attributed it to sin. The war
within him was sin versus righteousness. Paul
was fighting a lost war because he was not fighting
it in the power of Jesus Christ. Tried as he might
to conquer the sin that was ruling him, he was
always falling flat on his face in defeat and shame.
He would get up again, determined as ever, to
conquer this enemy and win the invisible war
within. But, the story never changed. It was a lost
cause.

He had been sold under sin, and sin had become
his master. This grip of sin was not about to let him
go. Jesus referred to this phenomenon in the
eighth chapter of John when He told the Jews,
"Verily, verily, I say unto you, Whosoever committeth
sin is the servant of sin, and the servant abideth
not in the house for ever: but the Son abideth ever."
(John 8:34-35) The Lord recognized the fact that
one may be under the dominion of sin. As a matter
of fact, the person who wishes to do what is right,

yet continually find himself falling short is a servant of sin.

The seriousness of this thought is expressed by prefixing it with "Verily." Jesus was dead serious about this concept. Sin is a master that is not about to let go any of his subjects. It will hold its victim in the callousness of its grips. Sin is a powerful master, and it is no respecter of person. Paul found this to be true. Peter was no exception. Adam was the first to taste its bitter truth. Sin is an enemy that fights within. It is a battle that is being raged right now within you. If the Christian has to be engaged in the war against sin, how then can it be overcome? What is the weapon? We have come to the conclusion that the weapon we need for the three battles are not physical weapons. But what weapon must be utilized for this war against sin? Is it the gifts of the Holy Spirit? Is it the working of miracles, or raising the dead, and healing the sick? No.

The spiritual weapon in this instance is not the gifts of the Spirit, but the fruit of the Spirit. God seeks to perfect us through suffering at times. There are some things that we must have to go through in order to overcome some areas of our lives. One of the fruit of the Spirit is longsuffering. Note that it does not say shortsuffering. It says and means longsuffering. You must have to suffer long in order to come out victorious. Our Lord and Predecessor learned obedience to God through the things that He suffered. His body recoiled at the idea of going to the cross.

Up to the last supper, He had suffered the rejection of the Jews. He had been excommunicated. He came unto His own, but His own were willing to cast Him headlong onto the precipice in their city. He had done miracles and performed healings among the multitude, but what He got in return was an attempt to stone Him.

Twice He fed the hungry supernaturally, but all they wanted was to take Him by force and make Him a King in order to deliver them from the oppression of the Romans. He cast out devils from the children of Israel, and instead of a grateful heart, the religious leaders of His day ascribed the exorcism to Beelzebub, the prince of devils.

At the last minute, one of His own inner twelve disciples, Judas Iscariot, sold Him for a slave's price to His enemies. Another close disciple was to deny Him three times before even a maid. The other disciples all forsook and fled when the soldiers came with spears to arrest Him. He was left alone.

As He prayed in the garden, He besought His disciples to pray with Him in this final battle. Instead, they slept. His agony was so intense, that blood flowed through his pores. For the first time, He asked God to reconsider the final suffering that must shortly take place. Was it the nails that He feared? No. Was it the mockery of the Sanhedrin and the soldiers that He recoiled at? That was great enough, but I do not believe that was the greatest suffering our Lord was facing.

The greater suffering was separation from His Father. He knew fully well that He would suffer separation from the Father. This was unknown to Him throughout His life time. Others might reject Him. His disciples might deny Him. His own people might take up stones to kill Him. He could take these. But separation from His heavenly Father was another thing.

His Father had been with Him all along. He Himself boasted that the Father had never left Him alone for He always did what His Father wanted Him to do. But now, as the Lamb of God that must be sacrificed to take away the sin of the world, our sin had to cause a temporary separation from His Father. With the Father's separation, so was also the separation of His strength. As He hung on the cross, suffering the physical agony, the greater agony was around the corner. He prayed, "Father, forgive them for they know not what they do." As the hours wore on, the Father saw the sin of the world on Him.

The nature of the Holy God could not behold sin, not even in His sinless Son. The Father forsook the Son, and the Son cried out, "Eloi, Eloi, lama sabathani ?" (Matt 15:34) Note that He did not say "Abba" He used the word, "Eloi" The El is the name of God in the Old Testament, and it means "The strong One" or "Strength." In an hour of suffering and weakness, the Lord turned to His strong One for strength through the suffering.

But through it all, He endured the suffering, He despised the shame, because He knew the many sons and daughters that He through His suffering would bring to glory, which include you and me. "For it became Him, for whom are all things, and by whom are all things, in bringing many sons into glory, to make the captain of their salvation perfect through sufferings." (Heb 2:10) How will you learn obedience without suffering? Many of us recoil at the prospect of suffering. We hate it with every atom of our being. But suffering must be present to be victorious. Perhaps, you are a bachelor. Do not pretend that you do not have sexual urges.

Do not claim spirituality by denying this normal and natural urge within you. If you do not have them, you are sick and a visit to the doctor is in order. Get a physical check-up. But when this sexual urge comes to you, you must deny yourself of fulfilling it. It will make you uncomfortable. It is a suffering, for you are not fulfilling that urge. But, if you want to be holy, you will have to suffer the denial of having sex. The alternative is to follow Paul's admonition. Get married. Perhaps you are a Christian. You are the object of ridicule of your old friends and colleagues. They ridicule your faith in an attempt to bring you back to your old ways. They entice you with drugs and alcohol. They remind you of the good old times when women were at your behest. They flash dollar bills before you and invite you to come with them to get it through illegal means as before. But, you must have to say no. Jesus says, "If anyone desires to follow me, let him deny Himself, take up his cross and follow me." (Luke 9:23)

When you deny yourself, this is what it means to suffer. Your flesh must not be allowed to have dominion over you, and that causes suffering and agony. Yes, you may have to be without money for awhile. Yes, you may not enjoy the temporary euphoria that drugs and alcohol provide. The suffering may seem unbearable, but remember the long run. Like the Captain of your salvation, Jesus Christ, who endured the cross "... for the joy that was set before him..." (Heb 12:2), you too, must look at the joy of being free from the shackles of these sins. You no longer need to suffer the side-effects of drugs and alcohol. You are shielded, to a great length, from contracting AIDS and other sexual diseases. You are spared from the general repercussions of sin. But above all, you have become the servant of righteousness and God. You now please God. You can sense His pleasure around you. Heaven lies within your bosom, for His will that is being done in heaven, is also being done in your life. For these joys and many more, you must endure the suffering. You must despise the shame. You must continue to stand for the righteousness of your God.

The fruit of the Holy Spirit also includes faith. Faith is a very powerful weapon. Paul equates it with a shield. With the shield of faith we quench the various darts of the enemy. (Eph 6:16) With the shield of faith, you are assured victory over sin, for sin is one of the fiery darts of the enemy.

One of the grievous things about the tactics of the enemy is guilt. Perhaps, you fell into sin. The enemy will want you to believe that God is through with you. He wants you to live in guilt and consequently deprive you of going to the throne room of God with confidence. But with the shield of faith, you are able to attack the enemy.

This faith will give you confidence in the shed blood of Jesus as the means of cleansing you. It will enable you to know that no matter how grievous your sin might be, if you confess it, God is faithful and just to forgive you and to cleanse you from all unrighteousness. (1 John 1:9-10) The shield of faith will help you to know that you are dead to sin. Your Savior has crucified sin in His flesh on your behalf. All you have to do is to believe and reckon yourself to be dead to sin also. This is the faith that conquers the allurement of the world. It is the faith that makes you realize that greater is He, [the Lord Jesus Christ], who is in you than He who is in the world. (1 John 4:4)

It is the faith that produces righteousness. The faith that Abraham had in God and which was accounted to him as righteousness. It is the faith that Moses wielded, that he refused to enjoy the pleasures of sin for awhile. It is the faith that pleases God (Heb 11:6). It is faith that believes that God is holy and to see Him, we must also avoid sin. The fruit of faith will shield you from the guilt and sin. If Adam and Eve had exercised faith in the commandment of God and refused to believe in the lie of the devil, it would have been a different story.

Are you constantly facing the fiery darts of the enemy? Do you feel powerless against the former sins in your life? Go and get the fruit of faith. Believe in the victory of Christ in your behalf. And if you sin, believe that if you confess your sins, God will forgive you. Believe every commandment that God gave to us in the New Testament as valid. You must have that faith that God does not condone sin, and He does not change His commandments. His commandments are changeless and deathless. Your faith in God to protect you will bring results. Believe that God is there for you. He wants to strengthen you with might by His Spirit in the inner man. Believe in His ever-abiding presence to protect you through the ups and downs of temptation.

Love is another fruit of the Spirit and a weapon. The Bible says we are to conquer evil with good. Jesus says to love even our enemies. Love also covers a multitude of sin. Indeed, love is the culmination of the commandment of God. You cannot abide in love and continue to sin. Loving

God is obeying Him, with all your heart, soul and strength.

With love in your heart, you do treat others the same way you want to be treated. The golden rule of our Lord Jesus Christ is to do unto others as we want them to do to us. He who loves will obey the commandments of God. Allow the love of God to saturate your heart. It will preserve you from sin.

If you feel you do not have this love, go to the One whose name is Love. God is love and that is where you can go and get love. He will give it to you copiously. At conversion, He has shed His love in your heart. Let it grow. Let it germinate. Let it be the rule of practice in your life. With love in your life, you will be patient with others. You will not be arrogant. With love, you will honor others above yourself, and you will not look down on your brethren because of their race, color, nationality and so on. Love is the strong antidote to forgiveness. Because you love, you are ready to forgive and will not laden others with your hurting remarks. Let the fruit of love overcome the fight of sin within your life.

The other fruits of the Spirit include joy, peace, gentleness, goodness, meekness and temperance. These fruits of the Spirit will conquer the lust of the flesh. These fruit of the Spirit and sin cannot cohabit. One will have to leave for the other. But you let the fruit of the Spirit dominate you.

Do not be a servant to sin, but be a servant of the fruit of the Holy Spirit. Let it be your master. Obey the dictates of the fruit of righteousness. When sin knocks at the door, send the fruit of the Holy Spirit. Let sin know that you are no longer its servant. You belong to another, and that is the Holy Spirit. This fruit is called the fruit of the Holy Spirit, because it is the Holy Spirit who enables you to produce them. Without the Holy Spirit living fully in your life, you cannot produce this fruit. Hence, you cannot afford to grieve the Holy Spirit.

You cannot afford not to be filled with the Holy Spirit either. You must not displease Him for He is the enabler within you fighting against sin. The Holy Spirit, the mighty Third Person of the Holy Trinity is all-powerful. He is the One who strengthens you with might in the inner person. Move with the flow of the Spirit. Allow the love of God that was shed abroad in your heart by the Holy Spirit bring forth in abundance.

The fruit of the Holy Spirit is thus the weapon against the war of sin raging within you. Greater is the Holy Spirit within you. Sin will want to gain entrance and dominate you as before. But, with the fruit of the Holy Spirit, sin is fighting a lost cause. Sin will remind you of the "beautiful times" you once enjoyed with it, but the fruit of faith in God will refuse the pleasures of sin which leads to death, and believe God that true pleasure and fulfillment are found in God.

Sin will tell you to be proud and have a superiority complex, but the fruit of meekness will remind you that sin originated with the pride of Lucifer who wanted to be above God. Sin may bring sorrow to wear you down and thus leave you powerless, but the fruit of joy will proclaim its strength, for the joy of the Lord is your strength. Sin will entice you to do evil to people, injuring their feelings and making them miserable, but the fruit of goodness is there to overcome evil with good. Sin will tell you to be afraid of the circumstance around you, for in doing so the boat might sink in the middle of the storm. But the fruit of peace that guarded the heart of our Lord in the midst of the storm, while the disciples panicked, will guard your heart.

Thank God we are not powerless. We have the fruit of the Holy Spirit to fight the war within us. We are more than conquerors through Him who died for us. We are able to conquer sin. We are able to dominate sin. We are able to have it under our feet. We are able to do all things through Christ who strengthens us. Amen and Amen.

Chapter 6

The Battle for Souls - Second War

The second battle we fight is to win souls for our Lord. In the garden of Eden, Adam sold out our souls to the enemy. From henceforth, they were driven from the Garden of Eden from the presence of the Lord. Man had lost God. Man could no longer find God. All hope seemed lost. There was no man to redeem man back to God for everyone was born a servant to the devil through Adam, our progenitor.

But Jesus came. Thanks be to God! The first phrase of our Lord in the public after His temptation in the wilderness was "Repent, the kingdom of heaven is at hand." (Matt 4:17) God was not bringing His kingdom to the souls of men. Previously, it was the kingdom of satan in our souls. We were stationed in his camp and we belonged to him, not out of choice but out of force.

Jesus came out of the wilderness having conquered the enemy of our souls in various temptations, three of which are recorded. Like a general of the army, He came forth. Why did Jesus have to go to the wilderness to be tempted first? Because, Jesus had to conquer the enemy first before He could set us free. Remember that, man of his own free volition sold himself and his offspring to the devil. The devil thus became the god of this world and its king. (2 Cor 4:4) He set his rule here on earth, and from there he wages his war in the souls of men. His rule had been confirmed, and he never thought anyone could challenge him .... until Jesus came.

A battle became inevitable. Jesus came to reclaim for man what man had lost in the Garden of Eden. He came to usher in the kingdom of God and the former master, satan, was not about to let his slave go free. A battle ensued in the wilderness. Satan wanted Jesus to sell out to him as Adam had done. He tempted him at the vulnerable points. But Jesus was victorious. He came out of every test victorious. Having conquered the enemy in the secret, He came out in the public and began to proclaim to people that the kingdom of God is at hand, they must therefore repent.

The kingdom preaching for Jesus was both in words and in demonstration of the Holy Spirit. He told people about their sin and how He must take away the sin. He revealed to them the Father. But He also demonstrated to them that He was indeed the Savior that must come into the world. His messiahship was defended by His miracles. The display of the supernatural occupied a significant role in the ministry of our Lord. Without the gifts of the Holy Spirit, people will not believe. As a case in point, John the Baptist had been cast in prison for speaking against the unlawful union of Herod and Herodias. (Luke 3:19-20)

He stayed in prison, and possibly awaiting deliverance from the Messiah. Yet, the news of the miracles which Jesus performed had reached his ears. He was still unsure of this Messiah. Yes, he had seen the Holy Spirit like a dove descend on Him. He had pointed Him out to his disciples as the Lamb of God that must take away the sin of the world. Indeed, he had baptized Him with water against the protest of his own unworthiness to baptize the Son of God. But, he remained in doubt. Unable to continue further, he sent his disciples to Jesus with the question, "Art thou He that should come, or do we look for another?." (Luke 7:19)

Jesus did not send a verbal confirmation to John. What Jesus did was to perform a few miracles before the disciples of His forerunner, John. He knew that it took miracles to convince John and encourage his heart. After the miracles, Jesus now turned to the disciples, and told them to carry the news of what they had just witnessed to their master, John. (Luke 7:21-22) Although, the Bible does not record the response of John to the message, I believe that his faith must have been strengthened in the fact that Jesus was indeed the Messiah that should come into the world. If John needed to see miracles to confirm the messiahship of Christ, how much more the sinners? Jesus needed to perform miracles to make men believe in Him as the Messiah and thereby be born into the kingdom of God.

The Samaritan woman saw Jesus at the well. Jesus asked her to give Him water to drink. The woman was rather reluctant to give Jesus a drink because of the hatred that existed between the Jews and the Samaritan. (John 4:7-9) Jesus began to preach to her. But he did more than preaching, He told her about her life. The woman then perceived that Jesus must have been a prophet. (John 4:19)

After the conversation of our Lord with this woman, the Bible records that the main reason why this woman was convinced that Jesus was the Messiah was because of the gift of prophecy or word of knowledge that Jesus displayed. In her own words, she told her countrymen, " Come, see a man, which told me all this that ever I did: is not this the Christ?" The miracle of knowing her personal life convinced her that Jesus was indeed the Christ. (John 4:29) Not long after this incident, the display of miracles was to be another basis for faith in Christ. An unnamed noble man had heard about the miracles of Jesus, especially the one he did in Cana of Galilee where He had turned water into wine. This was the same city that this noble man lived. His son was ill, about to die. All hope was lost.

As a noble man, he must have spent a lot of his resources to procure the healing of his son. But, there was no help for him. He was at the point of death when fortunately, Jesus visited his town again. This time, hope had arrived. He went to Jesus personally, and began to beseech Jesus to heal his son. And Jesus made an interesting remark, "Except ye see signs and wonders, ye will not believe: (John 4:48) The son of course was healed. But the remark of the Lord shows the need for signs and miracles.

The miracles of Jesus must always be viewed in their proper light. Miracles are supposed to be signs that point to the salvation that can be found only in the Son. On occasion, Jesus fed the multitude supernaturally. In this particular instance, with five loaves and two fishes, a company of five thousand men, not counting their wives and children had been fed to the fill. The Jews misunderstood this miracle.

Jesus corrected their mistaken notion that the miracle He did was a sign for them to accept Him as the Messiah of the world. Miracles brought souls to our Lord from every quarter. Seeing the miracles that Jesus did, these sinners knew that Jesus was indeed the Messiah. The gifts of the Spirit set seal of approval on Jesus Christ as the Messiah of the Jews and the Savior of the world. The dead were raised, the sick healed, the lepers were cleansed, and the sinners received forgiveness of sins. The demoniacs were delivered, the storm was stilled. It was the gifts of the Spirit that Jesus displayed that even made His disciples to believe Him. One of the last miracles that Jesus did and which brought the bitterest attack on him was the raising of Lazarus.

Jesus told His disciples that He was glad for their sakes that He was not there for now the disciples would witness another spectacular miracle - that of the raising of the dead Lazarus. Even the disciples needed continual re-affirmation of their faith in Christ as the Messiah. (John 11:15, 27, 40)

When Jesus was about to leave the earth, He told the disciples to wait for the promise of the Father, the Holy Spirit. (Acts 1:4) The Holy Spirit was given to reveal the Father unto men through Christ Jesus. The Holy Spirit was to equip them with boldness and power to demonstrate that Jesus was indeed this Messiah. The gifts of the Holy Spirit were to be displayed for people to believe.

Indeed, Jesus said that as those who believed in Him, they too would do the works of miracles that He did. They too would raise the dead, heal the sick, cleanse lepers. They would be able to lay hands on the sick and they would recover. They would drink poison, and it would not harm them. They would step on snakes and they would not be hurt. That was a heritage that Christ bequeathed His church. They were to continue in His footsteps. He used His word of mouth and miracles to win souls, and we too must engage in the same.

The early church witnessed the conversion of souls because of the miracles. For example, with the healing of the crippled man at the Beautiful gate, another two thousand souls were birthed into the kingdom. (Acts 3:6-8) The Sanhedrin were powerless to refute this miracle that turned the heart of the Jews to Jesus Christ. Miracles occurred frequently. The disciples employed this weapon to bring souls to the kingdom of God.

It was the gifts of miracles that won Samaria to the saving knowledge of Christ. Simon, a sorcerer had performed magic for a long time in Samaria. He bewitched the people of his area with magic and sorcery and witchcraft. But, when Philip came to Samaria, Simon witnessed authentic miracles, and signs which were done. For that reason, the sorcerer also believed. "Then Simon himself believed also: and when he was baptized, he continued with Philip, and wondered, beholding the miracles and signs which were done." (Acts 8:13) That is the power of the gifts of the Holy Spirit in the battle for souls. Some people will not believe unless they witness the supernatural.

When Paul was sent out on His first missionary journey, he was equipped with the gifts of the Holy Spirit. Paul was to contend with another sorcerer, this time in Paphos. Elymas, who was also Barjesus was a Jew, yet he practiced witchcraft. When Paul was brought before Sergius Paulus, a prudent man, Elymas tried to oppose Paul's message of Salvation. But, Paul proclaimed the judgement of God on him, and immediately Elymas became blind. Elymas now had to look for someone to lead him out.   The result was that Sergius Paulus believed. "Then the deputy, when he saw what was done, believed...." (Acts 13:12)

It was also the display of the gifts of the Holy Spirit that brought many to the saving knowledge of Jesus Christ. A viper had fastened itself on Paul's hand, but its venom did not kill Paul. The supernatural power of God kept Paul alive. Shortly after the incident, Paul healed the father of the chief man Publius of fever through the gifts of healing. Before long, others brought their sick folks as well and they were all healed.

Paul did not need to do much preaching. Later, he was to write to the Corinthians that when he came to them, it was in also in demonstration of spirit and of power of God. The early church was in tune with God. They knew they needed the gifts of the Holy Spirit to point the dying world to the Savior.   They continued in the path their Lord Himself had trodden, the path of the supernatural. With the Word of God and the gifts of the Holy Spirit, they demonstrated to the world that Jesus is indeed the Messiah, the One who would save them from their sins.

Many today do not see the relevance of spiritual gifts. They are for one thing; they are too lazy to seek God until God seals their preaching with signs following. Others believe that the age of miracles is past. They attribute the power of the supernatural to the past. To them, God is not interested in healing the people supernaturally. Instead, God has raised up medical crew to eradicate sickness. Yet, we know that as advanced as the medical technology has become, many continue to die of various illnesses. The gifts of healings have been relegated to the background of modern technology. Besides, the healing of the sick by medical technology does not point to the lordship of Christ.

I am a firm believer in medicine. I send people to the hospital. But healing from medicine is not a sign of the messiahship. It must not and will not supplant the supernatural gifts of the Holy Spirit that will point to the Savior. Some theologians believe that the early church needed the supernatural gifts of the Holy Spirit to start the church. But, if the church was founded on the miraculous, why should it not continue in the miraculous. In an age where the supernatural is viewed as a superstition, Christians need to prove to the world that Jesus is the Messiah. Miracles still happen. Miracles need to take place. Unbelievers are out there, who would not believe unless they see miracles. The church must continue to shine as the beckon light in a world that languishes in agony and suffering. The gifts of healings are still available to heal that terminal cancer and incurable AIDS. The word of knowledge (1 Cor. 12:8) is still needed to reveal the heart of the sinner, thereby bringing him to the saving knowledge of Jesus Christ. The gift of discerning of spirit is still needed to guide the church against the false spirit that wants to emulate the gifts of Christ. These gifts must be in operation to continue to win the lost to the saving knowledge of Christ.

The battle for the lost continues to rage. Heaven is open to receive as many as would accept Christ. Hell is reluctant to give up its present and future victims. There is nothing we can do about those who have died and are now in hell. Their fate is sealed. Their opportunity is gone, their death has been cast. But we can do something about the living who are bound on the way to hell. We must tell them about the saving knowledge. With some, presenting the Gospel of Jesus Christ is enough to convince them, with others, they must witness the gifts of the Holy Spirit. Which ever way, we must rescue the perishing. We must enlist in the army of the Lord to win souls to the kingdom. We must be faithful at the post of delegation.

The zeal of God must consume us. This is not a battle for the few; it is a battle that we all engage in. We must fight with the help of our God. We must set free the captives from their captor, the devil. We must swing open the gates of prison for the prisoners to be free. We must open the eyes of the blind with the light of the Gospel. We must take the Gospel of Christ to the four corners of the earth. We must tell the Islamic world that Jesus Christ is the Savior of the World. We must have to prove it with the supernatural gifts of the Holy Spirit. We must tell them that Jesus was not just a prophet, but the Son of the living God, and that there is no other name, under heaven, given among men, whereby we must be saved.

We must tell the Communist world that Jesus is the answer. We must demonstrate to them that there is another aspect of man that yearns for the Creator. Life is more than physical. There is a spiritual realm that is as real as the physical. We must tell them that the answer does not lie with Lenin or Marx. The answer to human suffering lies in Jesus Christ.

We must tell the atheists who do not believe either in God or in the supernatural that indeed there is God, and that this God is alive and well. His hand is not shortened that it can no longer perform miracles. The unseen God of the Universe is real and valid. With the gospel of Jesus Christ with signs following, some of these atheist will no longer have a hiding place. Let us go to every corner with this message of hope. There is hope for the lost. There is peace for the troubled. There is power to heal the sick. There is an antidote to depression and sadness. There is, above all, escape from hell through the name of Jesus Christ. Are you willing to go out there and win the lost to the Lord your God? Are you ready to show them the only way to heaven? If so, then you must not relent in your effort to continue to wage the battle against the kingdom of satan who does not want to give up. But, with the Lord Jesus Christ on our side, victory is ascertained.

Chapter 7

The Battle Against Sin - The Third War

The final war, is the war in which we engage with satan and his cohorts. This war is not the war in you, nor the war against satan's works, but the war directed at satan himself.

For we wrestle not against flesh and blood, but against principalities, against powers, against the rulers of the darkness of his world, against spiritual wickedness in high places. Wherefore take unto you the whole amour of God, that ye may be able to withst

and in the evil day, and having done all, to stand. Stand therefore, having your loins girt about with truth, and having on the breastplate of righteousness; And your feet shod with the preparation of the gospel of peace; Above all, taking the shield of faith, wherewith ye shall be able to quench all the fiery darts of the wicked.   Take the helmet of salvation, and the sword of the Spirit, which is the word of God: Praying always with all prayer and supplication in the Spirit, and watching thereunto with all perseverance and supplication for all saints. (Eph 6:12-19)

Paul said we are to take on the whole amour of God. We cannot fight the battle with the amour of man, but the amour of God. Without this amour, we are powerless and fall prey to the wiles of the enemy. Our enemy is the devil. He is not your friend but your bitter enemy. He hates you with all his guts, and all he cares for is your misery and separation from God. You cannot bargain with the enemy, for he will fool you. He has no need of you, except to use you and then dump you in hell. He is the father of lies. He will want to divert your attention from himself and direct your attention to flesh and blood who are not really the enemies.

In the western world, he has managed to fool some intellectuals who refuse to believe in the reality of wicked spirits. In your own might, you have no power against him. He does not dwell in the physical realm where you can see his ugliness and wickedness. He dwells in the heavenlies, and he is there, with his cohorts, to stop your prayers from being answered. He is there to make sure that you do not make heaven. He is there to intercept your walk with God. He is there to see that you do not maintain a close relationship with God. He is there to stop your worship with God.

God has not left you defenseless. When you gave your life to Christ, you became a soldier of Jesus Christ. You became enlisted in His army. You became his soldier. As a soldier, you must be armed. This amour has been provided for you, for you cannot manufacture it. However, you must put it on, not a part, because the enemy will attack at the exposed part. This amour, being God's amour, is sufficient for our defense as well as our offence. This amour, when put on, will assure certain victory. It is the amour of the Almighty God and therefore it is effective. Put on the whole amour of God, and be ready to defeat satan and his cohorts. They are powerful, but their power is rendered useless in the face of the Christian who is armed with the amour of the Almighty God.

This amour is put on to fight spiritual battles. Our enemies are really not men. Your brother is not your real enemy. Your boss is not the real enemy of your soul. The battle is not in terms of guns and missiles. The battle is against unseen forces. These forces cannot be seen with physical eyes, they are nonetheless tangible and real.

Paul now names some of the enemies in the kingdom of satan. They are numerous and they are energetic and active. They are also very furious. They have no mercy but, praise God, we have power over them in the mighty name of Jesus. Notice there is no amour for the back parts. In essence, there is no time to retreat. To retreat is to spell your defeat, for you are not protected when you turn your back on the enemy. Notice that Paul emphasized the need to stand. He mentioned it four times in this chapter. You must hold your ground. You must be steadfast in what the Bible has to say. Do not be swayed by every wind of doctrine that comes your way. You must stand your ground, and not be pushed here and there by the traditions of men.

You must stand in the liberty of which Christ has set you free. You must stand your ground in moments of temptation and discouragement. As a faithful soldier of Christ, you must stand your ground against the devil. Instead, you must oppose his assaults and his strategies. You must resist him, and he will flee from you. Now Paul takes us to different parts of the amour. Not to be protected in a given part is to be defeated, for each part is essential. The first one that Paul mentioned is the girdle.

In the Roman soldier, the girdle was not a decoration. It was indispensable, for it holds together the other parts of the armory. The girdle holds every part of the amour in place, therefore it is mentioned first. The girdle represents truth. Let truth cleave to you as a girdle. God desires truth in the inward parts. A Christian who tells lies is being opened to attacks of the enemy.

Some Christians make it a habit to tell lies once in a while. They do not see anything wrong in telling innocent lies. No lie is innocent. Lies are opposed to God and it is an attribute of the enemy. The devil cannot abide in truth for he is the father of lies. (John 8:44) What portion does a Christian have in lies? None. It is impossible for our God to tell lies. (Hebrews 6:18) Jesus Christ calls Himself the Truth, and the Holy Spirit is called the Spirit of Truth. (John 14:6, 16:13)

You have no business telling lies. Quit it! If you want to fight the devil successfully, you must tell the truth at all times. The truth may also refer to the truths of the gospel. You must hold on to the doctrines that are in the Bible, and not be swayed by different doctrines.

The next part of the amour is the breastplate of righteousness. A breastplate protects the heart and the other vital organs. The breastplate does not focus on the arm or leg, for the wound might heal. But it protects the heart because there may be a fatal consequence if the heart is wounded. Once the arrow pierces through the heart, the soldier is wounded, and may die.

The heart is the center of your life. If the enemy can get to the heart, he knows that your death is a matter of time. Do not allow satan to get into your spiritual heart. The weapon to use, is the righteousness of Christ. John, the beloved, wrote in his first epistle that we are not to sin, but if we sin, we have and advocate with the Father, the Lord Jesus Christ, who is our righteousness. This righteousness is by faith in Jesus Christ.

Know that you are covered with the righteousness of Christ. He is the One who died that you might now be righteous before God. Your own righteousness outside of Christ is described as filthy rags. (Isaiah 64:6) But your righteousness in Christ is like a breastplate. When the enemy comes to accuse you of a past sin, tell him that you have been covered with the breastplate of righteousness that Jesus has given to you. You become fortified against his attack and accusations. You tell him that it is God who justifies, and the enemy cannot condemn you.

This breastplate is also a reference to your own dedication to do what is right. A good conscience and integrity are necessary to remain a true soldier of Christ. When a Christian sins all the time, or he does not have respect for righteousness, he is opening his spiritual heart to the enemy. Once he gets in, he will work all kinds of sins in the believer's life. Peter lamented over Ananias because the latter allowed satan to fill his heart because he was not truthful. " But Peter said, why hath satan filled thine heart to lie to the Holy Ghost and to keep back part of the price of the land? (Acts 5:3)

Jesus said that it is the pure in heart who will see God. The state of your heart therefore determines whether you see God or not. But if your heart lies exposed, and the enemy who wants to deprive you of your relationship with God, gets in, you become wounded, and your relationship with God is in jeopardy. Put on then the breastplate of righteousness. It will protect and shield your heart from the intruder.

The feet are to be shod with the preparation of the gospel of peace. The feet must be well anchored if the soldier is to stand well. The feet must not be bare for they need firm footing when the devil attacks. With our feet, we advance with the gospel of peace. We take with us the gospel to the ends of the earth, for it is the power of God unto salvation to those who believe. We must hold fast the simple message of salvation and not be deviated by the devil. You must adhere to the tenets of the Gospel for no other person or angel who comes with another gospel must be believed.

It is also a gospel of peace. Let your life be characterized by peace. The writer of Hebrews says that as much as it lies within you, leave peaceable with all men. (Hebrews 12:14) But if the people will not believe the gospel of peace you bring to them, then, as the Lord told the disciples on the mission, let your peace remain with you. (Matt 10:13)

The message we carry is that of reconciliation. It is a message that the holy God is ready to have peace with us through Jesus Christ. Having peace with God, you may now enjoy a peace that passes all understanding. And with this inner peace, you are better able to live peaceably with others. Let your feet be shod with the good news of peace to all men.

The most important piece of this armory is the shield of faith. With the shield of faith you are able to quench the fiery darts of the wicked one. The fiery darts signify the desperation and wickedness of satan. They are darts like missiles. They are so fast, you cannot follow each move. The wounds that these darts inflict are very sharp on the flesh. The darts do not stop, for the wicked one will continue to throw these fiery darts on us. The darts are described as fiery and are blazing hot. The darts are fired to burn you up and destroy you. They will want to quench your zeal and faith in God. They will attack your love for God and quench your thirst for spiritual things.

But with the shield of faith, you are able to quench these fiery darts. The shield in the ancient times, and which Paul was referring to, could be as big as a door. It covered the entire length and width of the body. In fact, with the shield, you could not see the front, you must therefore hide behind this shield of faith. You must walk, not by the sight of the darts, but by faith.

The fiery darts come in different ways. Some fiery darts may be launched to destroy your faith in the holy scriptures. If you do not understand some things in the Bible, or you see some seeming contradictions, trust God to send you the answer at His own time, and hide behind the shield of faith in the truthfulness and infallibility of the Scriptures.

When the wicked one shoots his fiery darts on your weak points, hide behind the shield. Perhaps, you get angry easily or you are the jealous type, and the enemy will continue to fire those darts furiously and rapidly. Use the shield of faith to be able to render them powerless. But tell the devil that the good work that the Lord has begun in you, He is able to preserve it. Tell him that your God is able to save to the uttermost those who come to Him through Jesus Christ. God has promised that no weapon that is fashioned against you shall prosper, for that is your heritage and your righteousness is of God. Believe in the Lord, who is your shield and hiding place, to help you to overcome every besetting sin.

If the shield of faith is the antidote to the fiery darts of the enemy, then, you need to feed your faith. You must make sure that it is in good shape. How do you do this? Let the Word of God dwell in you richly. The Word of God is the seed that germinates faith. Without the Word of God, there is no foundation for faith. So build up your faith by allowing your mind to dwell on the Word.

The next weapon is the helmet of salvation. The helmet protects the head. No suit or armory is completed without a protection of the head. Your mind must know the truth about your salvation. You must know what the Bible has to say about every stage of your salvation. The helmet also enables you to look up in the heat of temptation, for your redemption draws near. The hope of our salvation enables us to know the reason for our hope in Christ Jesus.

Paul now moves to the offensive weapon. So far, Paul has been talking about defensive weapons, but now, he introduces the offensive weapon, which is the Word of God. It is called the sword of the spirit because all the Scriptures are given by the inspiration of the Holy Spirit. Jesus said that the words that He spoke were spirit and life. (John 6:63)

With this sword of the spirit you can attack the enemy. Jesus spoke the word of God and demons were cast out, the sick were healed, and other miracles took place. With the Sword of the Spirit, Jesus conquered the devil in the wilderness of temptation, the response of the Lord was seasoned with the sword of the spirit. He would say, "It is written." The captain of our salvation wielded this weapon in time of temptation, and the weapon continues to be available.

If you wield the sword of the spirit, you will be a terror to the enemy, for the Word of God cannot return to Him empty without accomplishing that for which you sent it. It will pierce through the spiritual darkness. It will attack the enemy of your soul, for he cannot stand in the presence of the flaming sword. The Word of God is likened to the flaming sword at the entrance of the Garden of Eden, which is to keep the intruders out.

Is the enemy battering you? Is he oppressing you with depression, sickness, and the like? Get out the sword of the spirit, and begin to confess what is yours through Jesus Christ. Let the Word of God do your battle for you. Let it be in your mouth, and let it abide in your heart. It will conquer the enemy of your soul.

Do you have the whole armory of God? Are you armed in every part? Are some parts vulnerable to the attack of the enemy? Do you even know what it means to be armed? Are you a wounded soldier? Has the enemy attacked you heart because you did not put on the breastplate of righteousness? Did you fail to put on the shield of faith, and consequently, the fiery darts of the enemy have wounded you, and you have fallen from your post? Maybe, your walk has been impeded because your feet were not shod with the preparation of the gospel of peace. Whatever the case, you can rise up again. There is hope for your future.

Go to God and prayerfully put on each part of His armor. Consciously place on your head, the hope of salvation. Fasten your waist with the girdle of truth. Put on your chest, the breastplate of righteousness, and be shod with the preparation of the Gospel of peace. Bring out of the sheath the sword of the Spirit, and with it attack the enemy of your soul. God has provided the armor, put it on!

Chapter 8

Worship in the Church

The worshippers are the closest to God. If you want to hear God's voice, be a worshipper. We can prophesy because God has imparted His thoughts in our hearts which we, in turn, translate into words. To prophesy, you need to hear from God.

Satan was a worshipper. He used to be, what we call, the choir master. He used to stay day and night before God, and simply worship Him. As a worshipper, he knew the mind of God. When you worship God, you touch His heart. God loves to be praised. He commands all living things to praise Him. "Let everything that hath breath praise the Lord." (Psalms 150:6) There is something in the nature of God that desires praise. As the Creator, all things are made for His pleasure. His pleasure includes praising Him. Jesus told the Samaritan woman, "God is a spirit, and they that worship him must worship him in spirit and in truth." (John 4:24) For of such, the Father seeketh. God is seeking worshippers. He loves to be worshipped. Hence, prophesy often comes in the midst of praise.

Satan was a worshipper. He gained access to the presence of God. As a worshipper He began to get a glimpse of the mind of God. Thank God, not all of it. He knew of what God was thinking of the human race. He did not like the plan. He knew that God was going to make another species, this time, in His own image. This species will be called man. Unlike angels, they would be made in the image of God. God was going to come down and commune with them. Satan opposed the idea. How could he sabotage that plan? In fact, how could he become God himself, an object of praise and worship? Then, he would be the Most High, and do as he would choose. He decided to be like God. And therein lay his fall. The Bible graphically describes how this worshipper fell through pride.

How art thou fallen from heaven, O Lucifer, son of the morning? How art thou cut down to the ground, which didst weaken the nations! For thou hast said in thine heart, I will ascend into heaven, I will exalt my throne above the stars of God: I will sit also upon the mount of the congregation, in the sides of the north: I will ascend about the heights of the clouds: I will be like the Most High. Yet thou shalt be brought down to hell, to the sides of the pit. (Isaiah 14:12-15)

Such was the downfall of one of the archangels. He was able to get one third of the angels to follow him. They fell for his lie, and decided to rebel. Jesus said that the devil was a liar from the beginning and abode not in truth. (John 8:44) But

Michael brought back order in heaven. He went into battle with Lucifer and his angels, and Michael and his angels won. Satan was cast down upon the earth. Now, there is a problem here on earth because Lucifer is here. Satan is not yet in hell, otherwise there would have been no problem on the earth.

Worship constitutes an important part in the church. The church is made for the glory of God. God still seeks worship. Man is made to worship God, for we are created for His glory, and He loves us to express our appreciation for what He has done for us. "Thou art worthy, O Lord, to receive honor and glory and power, for thou hast created all things and for thy pleasure, they are and were created." (Rev 4:11) We are to put on the garments of praise. Praise should not be relegated to the background of other things.

It is not a side issue. Praise is important to God. David, the man called, "the man after God's own heart," placed praise as one of the central issues in his life. He was willing to bless God at all times, and His praise was continually in his mouth. The purpose for gathering on Sunday morning is not to hear the Word. The chief purpose is to worship. The Scriptures say, "Come, let us worship and bow down, let us kneel before the Lord, today if you will hear his voice, harden not your heart." (Psalm 95:6) Notice that immediately, after a call to worship God, the next thought deals with hearing God's voice for the present. If you would not worship Him, you will not hear what He is telling you NOW. You will hear someone else's voice.

How important to hear what God has to say about our nation! Nothing will happen in your nation without God revealing it to you. Does God do anything without revealing it to his servants the prophets? God told Abraham what He was going to do to Sodom and Gomorrah because of Lot, Abraham's nephew, who was there. If the church would spend time worshipping our Father who is in Heaven, we too will not be left in darkness about our nation.

But the church is too busy. They have "better" and "more pressing" things to do. They come late to service, and are ready to leave early. They allot the time they will spend in service in praise to God. So, they leave their turkey or chicken in the oven with the timer on. When the service is underway, satan reminds them of their roast and they become fidgety. They are ready to go home. Go home to what ... to their roast, turkey or chicken?

How sad, that we do not have time enough to worship our Creator. The One who gave us breath and all that we have. Until the church gets back to worshiping God, nothing gets done. You must be ready to worship God as long as it takes for him to accept it. It is not enough to offer sacrifice of praise. Praise, by the way, is a sacrifice. It costs you to praise God. It costs you time and energy to praise God in the face of all odds. We keep on sacrificing praise to God until the frankincense ascends to God, and it becomes a sweet smelling savor.

One day in my church, we had worshipped and praised God for about two hours. Then the microphone was handed over to me to give the Word. But I heard the voice of God say that we had not praised Him enough. In obedience to the voice of the Lord, I called the church back to worship, which lasted another hour. Then the Lord was ready to give the Word for "today."

But some will murmur within themselves and complain that their turkey is burning. God is God and He has right to keep people as long as He wants. If they wish, they may dismiss themselves, but they must not hinder others by creating a critical spirit in the atmosphere. Praise begins on Saturday night on your bed. (Psalm 149:5) There are some people, who, when they arrive in church for service, you will need to shake them up for at least 30 minutes, so spiritually lethargic are they! By Sunday morning, you must be ready. Ready to praise God in spirit and in truth. The incense of praise and worship must be offered with the prayers of the saints. How many saints? All!

This is the reason why the church is weak because the incense was not offered with the prayers of the saint - only with a few. Only a few saints come to prayer meeting. The believers must worship God in unity and one purpose. The worship leader says it is time to lift up holy hands, but some feel it is time to put their hands in their pockets. They carry their rebellious spirit even to service. There must be unity in praise. If the worship leader says raise your hands, you should raise your hands, and if you do not have hands, raise up where they used to be. There is power in unity. We must loose ourselves in praise. Forget time. Forget people around you. Forget the boss you are going to meet on Monday. Forget the poor condition of your family. Loose yourself in praise to the Almighty. Praise Him with all your might. As David danced with all his might before his God, so must you praise and worship God with every ounce of your strength.

After loosening ourselves in praise and worship, then comes time to hear the Word of God for Today. He will speak, and we will hear His voice, as the Pastor teaches from the Word.

Chapter 9

The Holy Spirit in the Church

Jesus was leaving the disciples. He had taught them a lot of things, things that they could not fully grasp. He had revealed Himself as the Messiah that should come into the world, and they had believed in Him. Now, He was leaving them in order to return to His Father who had sent Him. But, He promised that He would send Someone, who would expatiate on what He had taught them. Many of the teachings of Jesus Christ to the disciples had not yet been understood, because they were not yet born again, since Jesus was not yet resurrected.

When the Holy Spirit, the third person of the Holy Trinity, arrives, He would not only bring into remembrance what He, Jesus, had told them but also help them to understand the truth.

The Teacher

The Holy Spirit is the Teacher of the church of Jesus Christ. "But the anointing which ye have received of him abideth with you, and ye need not that any man should teach you: but as the same anointing teaches you of all things." (1 John 2:27) This is a direct echo of what Jesus had told John and the rest of the disciples about the Holy Spirit. The Spirit will teach and enlighten our hearts to the Word of God. Remember that the Bible is inspired by the Holy Spirit.

The men who wrote down the words of the Bible might not have understood all that they were writing, but they were borne along by the Holy Spirit. And who is the best Interpreter of the Word, but the Holy Spirit. One day, the Lord spoke to me, "How come my people are not learning from their teacher?" They will not even talk to their teacher. If you don't talk to your teacher, how can you learn? Paul prayed for the Corinthians that they might have a communion with the Holy Spirit. "May the grace of your Lord Jesus Christ, and the love of God and the communion of the Holy Spirit, be with you all." (2 Cor 13:14)

The Greek text actually uses the word koinonia, which means fellowship. The translators of the KJV expressed it as "communion". You need to fellowship with the Holy Spirit. He is not a thing, or a force, He is a person. All that you need to learn about Jesus Christ, you need to depend on the Holy Spirit through the written Word to reveal to you. Every lesson that the Holy Spirit will give you will square with the Bible, because He is its author. So do not think you received a doctrine from the Holy Spirit that does not agree with the Bible.

By the same token, unless you depend on the Holy Spirit to teach you, you may know all the doctrines of the Bible, and still not profit from it. The disciples heard what Jesus had to say, but without the Holy Spirit in them, they could not grasp its meaning. The Pharisee, the Scribes and the Lawyers of Jesus' day knew the Scriptures. But, they did not understand them.

The Scripture was pointing to Christ, but without the Spirit, they were blind, and they failed to see who Jesus was. No wonder, when Nicodemus came to Jesus by night, Jesus told him that unless he was born by the Spirit, he cannot enter the Kingdom of God. If you are not in the kingdom, how can you understand the message of the kingdom. The Holy Spirit must be present to teach us the deeper things of God.

Tongues

With the coming of the Holy Spirit, comes the ability to speak the language of the Holy Spirit. The 120 disciples had gathered at the upper room in obedience to the Lord. (Acts 1:13-15) After ten days of being in harmony and prayer, the Holy Spirit, the promised One from the Father and the Son, was poured out on the church. They began to speak with new tongues. They began to speak about the goodness of God in the various languages of the devout men and women who had gathered in Jerusalem to celebrate Pentecost. (Acts 2:6) When the Holy Spirit was given, He enabled men and women to speak His language. He is still the same. If you allow Him, He will give you a language that you do not understand.

This language is not the language of the world. It is the language of the Spirit. It is the language given to the church by the Holy Spirit. The church is a nation, "But you are a royal generation, a royal priesthood, a holy nation, that ye should declare the works of him who has called you from darkness into his marvelous light." Each nation has its own language. The English nations speak English. The German nations speak German, The French nation speak French. The spiritual nation must also speak a spiritual language.

There are some spiritual languages that are known while others are totally unknown, except to the Father. For example, on the day of Pentecost, the empowered disciples spoke in a language that, although foreign to them, were known by others, whose languages they supernaturally spoke. Although the language is given in the spiritual realm, they did exist in the natural realm. There are some languages that can be given through the interpretation of the Holy Spirit. Yet there are some spiritual languages that the Holy Spirit does not give us its interpretation. That is why, some Pentecostals call speaking in tongues, a prayer language.

Thus, there is a speaking in tongue known only to the Father. The devil does not know the language so that he cannot understand it and attempt to hinder it. I can talk to my Father, and the devil is not able to understand it. That is one of the reasons we engage in warfare. There is a code language that is known only to some people. The enemy cannot understand the language. Hence, spies are sent to decode it. It is a strategy of warfare. We are engaged in a warfare and we are in it to win! When things are difficult, and the enemy surrounds me, I simply get into the unknown code, so that the purpose of the enemy is thwarted.

Chapter 10

The Church and the End Times

The Kingdom of this world has become the Kingdoms of our Lord, and of His Christ; and He shall reign forever and ever.
Revelation 11:15

As we are propelled by the motion of time into the twenty-first century, the role that the Church will play in society will become more aggressive, more assertive, more involved and extremely more evident and obvious than it ever has in its history of existence. The Bible declares that as we get closer to the culmination of the end times things in the earth will grow darker and darker, and circumstances and problematic conditions will get worse and worse. Jesus said that the love of many shall wax cold and the hearts of men, just as it was in the days of Noah will become all the more wicked and evil.

The Apostle Paul in 2 Timothy 3: 1-5, said that in the last days would be perilous times. "For men shall be lovers of their own selves, covetous, boasters, proud, blasphemers, disobedient to parents, unthankful, unholy, without natural affection, trucebreakers, false accusers, continent, fierce, despisers of those that are good; Traiters, heady, high-minded, lovers of pleasures more than lovers of God; Having a form of godliness, but denying the power therof: from such turn away." In contrast to this, the Bible declares the candle of the Lord in the heart of the born-again believers will grow and glow brighter and brighter. The distinction between the righteous and unrighteous will very most obvious.

In reaction to this wickedness, Paul went on to say in verse 12, that all those who live Godly will suffer persecution. (verse 13) But continue thou in the things which thou hast learned and hast been assured of. Therefore the Church is faced with two major challenges in the end times. One is to remain Godly and faithful to righteousness, even in the face of much wickedness and grave persecution. The second thing is to be fervently, actively involved in the work of evangelizing the world for the purpose of bringing souls into the Kingdom of God and out of them disciples of God and His Christ. This is basically the work of "Ambassadorship," reconciling man back to God.

Kingdom Ambassadors - Representatives of Christ and His Kingdom

All this is from God, who reconciled us to himself through Christ and gave us the ministry of reconciliation: that God was reconciling the world unto

Himself through Christ, not counting men's sins against them. And He has committed to us the message of reconciliation. We are therefore Christ ambassadors, as though God were making His appeal through us. We implore you on Christ's behalf: Be reconciled to God.

God made Him who had no sin to be sin for us, so that in Him we might become the righteousness in God. 2 Cor 5:18-21 NIV

God is going to judge the world by the standard of the Church. In these last days, as God continues to shake every kingdom and nation that is not built upon the foundation of His word, the Church must now begin to truly show forth the glory of God.

Not by just mere oratory and verbal teaching and preaching, but we must manifest the will of God by and through our every action. And when declaring the truth of Gods word we must articulated in such a way that it is relevant to the issues that are presently plaguing mankind. We must as wise ambassadors, make the rulers aware of the policies and dictates of God and his kingdom as they relate to the issues of the day.

The world must be made aware that in the midst of all the turmoil, destruction, hopelessness and confusion, there is a physical as well as spiritual entity in the earth that has solid and effective answers. And that entity is exclusively and only the Church community, the ecclasia.

A Kingdom Witness

And this gospel of the Kingdom shall be preached in all the world for a witness unto all nations; and then shall the end come.
Matthew 24:14

I have heard many preachers and Christians say "All I know is Jesus Christ and Him crucified." And my response to such a remark is if that is so, you only know the basics...It's fundamental and you must have that, "Jesus Christ and Him crucified," but it's not all there is to the true Christian message. Many people speak of Christ's immediate return, as if though it may happen tomorrow. Well I disagree with that line of thinking. Why? Because Jesus said that before His imminent return there are certain things that must take place. And one major event that is to take place in this sequence of events is that the gospel of the Kingdom would be preached for a witness unto all the world and unto every nation. The gospel of the Kingdom is not the same as the gospel of salvation. The gospel of salvation is basically in its simplest form, "Jesus Christ and Him crucified (and of course, rose again on the third day)."

The gospel of the Kingdom is in essence the total submission to the rule, government and sovereignty of God, Christ and His Kingdom. The Church's present job is now to colonize as many minds (souls), communities, cultures and nations as we possibly can in the allotted time we have remaining on earth.

This to be done firstly, by the proclamation of the Word in order to change the hearts and minds of men. Secondly, we must make our influence be felt in our communities by showing, through grass roots efforts our care and concern for fellow neighbors. We are our brothers keeper.

And thirdly, we must like the Apostle Paul take a bold and righteous stand against the prevalent wickedness of our day. We are to take a stand every regardless if it's in the White House or the out house.

In conclusion, we the body of Christ must embrace the God ordained reality that this is the Church's greatest hour. We need not get dismayed at all the troublesome things that plaguing the earth. The darker things get, the greater the Church will become in demand. We, who are leaders, must make sure that we take the necessary steps to begin to effectively equip the saints to handle and do all the evangelizing work that is about to be required of the Church. The future is literally in our hands. So let us like the great Patriarch general, Joshua, rise up and go possess the land.

OTHER BOOKS FROM

Pneuma Life Publishing

The Call of God $7.95
by Jefferson Edwards

Since I have been called to preach, Now What? Many sincere Christians are confused about their call to the ministry. Some are zealous and run ahead of their time and season of training and preparation while others are behind their time neglecting the gift of God within them. **The Call of God** gives practical instruction for pastors and leaders to refine and further develop their ministry and tips on how to nourish and develop others with God's Call to effectively proclaim the gospel of Christ.

The Call of God will help you to: • Have clarity from God as to what ministry involves • Be able to identify and affirm the call in your life •   See what stage you are in your call from God • Remove confusion in relation to the processing of a call or the making of the person • Understand the development of the anointing to fulfill your call.

Just Water $5.95
by T.D. Jakes

In this devotional and motivational book. Bishop T.D. Jakes inspires and motivates his readers to encourage themselves in the Lord by taking refuge in knowing God is able to provide even in the midst of impossible circumstances. Bishop Jakes provokes and invites us to rely on God's source of supply even in the wilderness. Noting that we must experience the wilderness before we can receive our inheritances. The purpose of the wilderness is for the purifying of our faith. And our faith makes us confident that God does indeed provide for our every need.

Why? *Because Your Are Anointed* $6.95
by T.D. Jakes

Why is it that the righteous, who have committed their entire lives to obeying God seem to endure so much pain and experience such

1 - 8 0 0 - 7 2 7 - 3 2 1 8

conflict? Why do many Christians often suffer while those who live by the dictate of the world seem to enjoy life and reap all the blessings? Why do bad things happen to good people? Why are the anointed persecuted? Why does the vision tarry? These are perplexing questions that plagued and bewildered Christians as well as unbelievers for ages. In this anointed and inspirational new book. "WHY," Bishop T.D. Jakes, the preacher with the velvet touch and explosive delivery, provocatively and skillfully answers these questions and many more as well as answering the "WHY" of the Anointed.

The Flaming Sword $6.95
by Tai Ikomi

Scripture memorization and meditation bring tremendous spiritual power, however many Christians find it to be an uphill task. Committing Scriptures to memory will transform the mediocre Christian to a spiritual giant. This book will help you to become addicted to the powerful practice of scripture memorization and help you obtain the victory that you desire in every area of your life. The Flaming Sword is your pathway to spiritual growth and a more intimate relationship with God.

Opening the Front Door of Your Church $9.95
by Dr. Leonard Lovett

A creative approach for small to medium churches who want to develop a more effective ministry. Did you know that 75% of churches in the United States have 150 attendance? Opening the Front Door of your Church is an insightful and creative approach to church development and expansion, especially for churches within the urban environment.

In this book Dr. Lovett... • Answers seven important questions that hold the key to maximizing effectiveness. • Explains the cost of following the Kingdom mandate. • Reveals how to open the front door while securing the sides and closing the back. • Illustrates Kingdom evangelization and liberation • Amplifies how your church can grow by being qualitatively oriented rather than numerically oriented.

1 - 8 0 0 - 7 2 7 - 3 2 1 8

This is My Story $9.95
by Candi Staton
This is My Story is a touching Autobiography about a gifted young child who rose from obscurity and poverty to stardom and wealth. With million-selling albums and a top-charting music career, came a life of heart-brokenness, loneliness and despair. This book will make you both cry and laugh as you witness one woman's search for success and love.

Single Life *A Celebration unto the Lord* $7.95
by Earl Johnson
A book that candidly addresses the spiritual and physical dimensions of the single life is finally here. Single Life shows the reader how to make their singleness a celebration rather than a burden. This positive approach to singles uses enlightening examples from Apostle Paul, himself a single, to beautifully portray the dynamic aspects of the single life by serving the Lord more effectively.

The book gives a fresh light on practical issues such as coping with sexual desires, loneliness and preparation for future mate.

Written in a lively style, the author admonishes the singles to seek first the Kingdom of God and rest assured in God's promise to supply their needs.... including a life partner!

Another Look at Sex $4.95
by Charles Phillips
This book is undoubtedly a head turner and eye opener that will cause you to take another close look at sex. In this book, Charles Phillips openly addresses this seldom-discussed subject and gives life-changing advice on sex to married couples and singles. If you have questions about sex, this is the book for you.

Beyond the Rivers of Ethiopia $6.95
by Dr. Mensa Otabil
Beyond the Rivers of Ethiopia is a powerful and revealing look into God's purpose for the Black Race. It gives scholastic yet simple answers to questions you have always had about the Black presence in the Bible. At the heart of this book is a challenge and call to the offspring of the Children of Africa both on the continent and throughout the world to come to grips with their true identity as

1 - 8 0 0 - 7 2 7 - 3 2 1 8

they go Beyond the Rivers of Ethiopia.

Four Laws of Productivity $7.95

by Dr. Mensa Otabil

In Genesis 1:28, God commanded man to do four things: (1) "Be fruitful, and (2) multiply, and (3) replenish the earth, and (4) subdue it: and have dominion .." In the past, many people read and thought that this scripture only meant to have many children. This scriptural passage is not confined to reproduction, but is the foundation for all productivity. The Four Laws of Productivity by Dr. Mensa Otabil will show you how to: Discover God's gift in you, develop the gift, and how to be truly productive in life. The principles revealed in this timely book will radically change your life.

Gifted - *Discovering Your Hidden Greatness* $8.95

by Jefferson Edwards

God has invested unique gifts and talent into every race and culture. In this book, the author calls attention to the particular gifts that God has bestowed on the Black race. In this book, you will gain fresh appreciation of the roles blacks played even in welcoming the King of glory to our cosmos. It is a call to the Black race to reach deep into their treasures and discover, develop and with excellence release their gift to the King. Now is the time, the author affirms, for fulfilling the prophecies, "Ethiopia (blacks) shall soon stretch out her hand unto God," and "the Kings of Sheba (blacks) shall offer gifts." The time is NOW!

The 1993 Trial on the Curse of Ham $6.95

by Wayne Perryman

For the past 300 years, many Western and European Scholars of Christianity have claimed that Ham, Noah's third son, and his Black descendants were cursed, and "[Blacks] would forever be servants to others." Over 450 people attended this trial. It was the first time in over 3000 years that Ham had an opportunity to tell his side of the story and explain exactly what took place in the tent of his father, Noah. The evidence submitted by the defense on behalf of Ham and his descendants was so powerful that it shocked the audience and stunned the jury. Evidence presented by the

1 - 8 0 0 - 7 2 7 - 3 2 1 8

defense was supported by over 442 biblical references.

Know the Truth $9.95
by James Giles

This book is an exciting journey into the rich African cultural heritage. It reveals unheard legacies of founding church fathers, biblical contributions of Ethiopia and other African countries, the technological advancement and innovations of early Africans and many other valuable gems of truth. In this book, James Giles approaches Black achievement with much research and comprehension. This book is part of the reeducating of not only African-American people but people of all cultures. Now you can also *Know the Truth.*

Strategies for Saving the Next Generation $5.95
by Dave Burrows

This book will teach you how to start and effectively operate a vibrant youth ministry. This book is filled with practical tips and insight gained over a number of years working with young people from the street to the parks to the church. Dave Burrows offers the reader vital information that will produce results if carefully considered and adapted. Excellent for Pastors and Youth Pastor as well as youth workers and those involved with youth ministry.

The Church A Mystery Revealed $7.95
by Turnel Nelson

Contrary to the popular and present image of the Church as a religious entity known as Christianity, God's purpose and intent for the Church is that its members be embassadors on earth that represent and manifest the policies, dictates and purposes of the Kingdom of God. In this book, Pastor Turnel Nelson addresses and outlines some of the fundamental measures that need to be taken in order to revitalize the Church for 21st century evangelism and discipleship.

Come, Let Us Pray   *by Emmette Weir*   **$6.95**

Are you satisfied with your prayer Life? Are you finding that your prayers are often dull, repetitive and lacking in spiritual power? Are you looking for ways to improve your relationship with God? Would you like to be able to pray more effectively? Then *Come, Let Us Pray* will help you in these areas and more. If you want to gain the maximum spiritual experience from your prayer life and enter into the very presence of God. *Come, Let Us Pray.*

Leadership in the New Testament Church   **$7.95**
by Earl D. Johnson

Leadership in the New Testament Church offers practical and applicable insight into the role of leadership in the present day church. In this book, the author explains the qualities that leaders must have, explores the interpersonal relationships between the leader and his staff, the leaders' influence in the church and society and how to handle conflicts that arise among leaders.

Becoming A Leader   **$9.95**
by Myles Munroe

Many consider leadership to be no more than staying ahead of the pack, but that is a far cry from what leadership is. Leadership is deploying others to become as good as or better than you are.

Within each of us lies the potential to be an effective leader. **Becoming A Leader** uncovers the secrets of dynamic leadership that will show you how to be a leader in your family, school, community, church and job.

Whereever you are or whatever you do in life this book can help you inevitably become a leader. Remember it is never too late to become a leader. As in every tree there is a forest, so in every follower there is a leader.

Becoming A Leader *Workbook*   **$7.95**
by Myles Munroe

Now you can activate your leadership potential through the *Becoming A Leader Workbook*. This workbook has been designed to take you step by step through the leadership principles taught in Becoming A Leader. As you participate in the work studies in this workbook you will see the true leader inside you develop and grow

1 - 8 0 0 - 7 2 7 - 3 2 1 8

into maturity. "Knowledge *with action produces results.*"

Mobilizing Human Resources $7.95
by Richard Pinder

Pastor Pinder gives an in-depth look at how to organize, motivate and deploy members of the body of Christ in a manner that produces maximum effect for your ministry. This book will assist you in organizing and motivating your 'troops' for effective and efficient ministry. It will also help the individual believer in recognizing their place in the body, using their God given abilities and talents to maximum effect.

The Minister's Topical Bible $14.95
by Derwin Stewart

The Minister's Topical Bible covers every aspect of the ministry providing quick and easy access to scriptures in a variety of ministry-related topics. This handy reference tool can be effectively used in leadership training, counseling, teaching, sermon preparation and personal study.

The Believers' Topical Bible
by Derwin Stewart

The Believers' Topical Bible covers every aspect of a Christian's relationship with God and man, providing biblical answers and solutions for all challenges. It is a quick, convenient, and thorough reference Bible that has been designed for use in personal devotions, and group bible studies. Over 3500 verses that are systematically organized under 240 topics, and is the largest devotional-topical Bible available in NIV and KJV.

New International Version $13.95 **KJ V $12.95**

The Layman's Guide to Counseling 9.95
by Susan Wallace

The increasing need for counseling has caused today's Christian leaders to become more sensitive to raise up lay-counselors to share this burden with them. Jesus' command is to "*set the captives free.*"

1 - 8 0 0 - 7 2 7 - 3 2 1 8

The Layman's guide to Counseling shows you how.

Topics Include: • Inner Healing • Parenting • Marriage • Deliverance • Abuse • Forgiveness • Drug & Alcohol Recovery • Youth Counseling • Holy Spirit • Premarital Counseling

A number of visual aids in the form of charts, lists and tables are also integrated into this reference book being the most comprehensive counseling tools available. The Layman's Guide to Counseling gives you the knowledge you need to counsel in advanced principles of Word-based counseling to equip you to be effective in your counseling ministry.

Books are available at your Local Bookstore or by contacting:

Pneuma Life Publishing

1-800-727-3218

1-805-324-1741

**P.O. Box 10612,
Bakersfield, CA 93389-0612**